North Charleston, SC

Library of Congress Control Number 2014905254

Create Space Title ID 4679641

ISBN 13 978-1496006370

Title: Forbidden Meteorology

Author: John Billen

North Charleston, SC

Library of Congress Control Number [illegible]

CreateSpace [illegible]

[illegible]

The [illegible]

[illegible]

Forbidden Meteorology

By John Billen

Dedicated to Bill Maher

Table of Contents

Introduction

Truth Surpasses all else in Beauty
JB

Meteorology is one of the younger sciences. The wise men and philosophers of long ago certainly noticed storms and drought, and the passing of the seasons. Without a rough topographical map of the Earth, only possible after the globe had been circled by travelers, could meteorologists properly conduct the working of that science. Early civilization was unaware the Earth was spherical in shape.

Some probably concluded that the Earth was a sphere. The idea that the Earth might be spherical must have occurred to people then, the Sun and Moon are spheres so the Earth would have seemed likely to be a sphere as well. Proof of the Earth's spherical nature, and its size, were lacking.

Knowing Earth's shape and dimensions, and its spin on its axis led to the discovery of the Coriolis effect, around 1835, that shows water running down a drain in the northern hemisphere does so counterclockwise, while in the southern hemisphere water will circle down a drain in a clockwise direction. The same kind of orientation is seen in storms. High pressure systems spin clock wise north of the equator, and low pressure systems spin counter clockwise there. The opposite applies to the southern hemisphere. There have been a few tornadoes in the northern hemisphere that spun clockwise, or span counter clockwise in the southern hemisphere, but only rarely, and only tornadoes, the structure of the rare tornado coming from a storm system of the proper orientation to its hemisphere. A cyclone could cross the equator from the southern hemisphere and keep spinning clockwise, possibly even intensify under the right conditions.

Meteorology involves electricity, and electricity wasn't very well understood until a long time after the globe had been traversed. Lightning, electric eels, magnetic rocks and static electricity have been observed by our species for a very long time, but knowledge of electricity goes back only 200 years or so. Lightning is a weather event involving electricity. Static electricity accumulates in clouds, some of which is eventually released as lightning.

The atomic structure of matter as it is now understood is also a fairly new discovery. Knowing the infinitesimally small size of atmospheric components is of great importance in learning anything about atmospheric events. The science of physics has gone far in the last century, identifying processes, the elements, and discerning the size of each. Inertia and how it works is well thought out. Wind, we now know, is quite a large collection of extremely small things traveling in the same general direction.

Aviation gives an investigator into meteorological events an enhanced perspective to observe clouds, and humans mastering flight is also a fairly recent event. Some television providers have a channel with a view of the Earth from space continually. A big difference between the current perspective on things and the more limited perspective of ancient times. If Confucius or Aristotle could see a satellite image of Earth now, he would be amazed by what everyday people currently find commonplace.

Astronomy, cosmology and astrophysics are also pretty new. The immense amount of astronomical data coming in daily from all the land telescopes, the Hubble telescope and other satellites in orbit is so far beyond what humanity was aware of in 3 to 5 hundred BC, the times of Confucius and Aristotle, that there is no comparison. During those times, cosmology and astrophysics didn't exist, and meteorology and astronomy were rudimentary at best. The ancients had no idea what the tiny lights in the sky at night were. Eventually constellations were named, and in time the tiny pin pricks of light were named stars, long before it was even realized that stars are suns, burning at millions of degrees.

Time marches onward, and the day will come when we are the primitives with limited vision. Two thousand more years will elapse, and civilization will certainly look back upon the era when humanity dealt with weather modification for the first time with some amusement. To them it will appear to have taken ancient humans 140 years to place a discovery made into Encyclopedia. Too timid to confront the issue for that long. Two thousand years hence, several new sciences will have developed from other disciplines, some from psychology, some from chemistry and physics, some from biology, perhaps a science of applied meteorology.

The skies are very well monitored on a continual basis in this day and age. New technology like Doppler radar make the observation of weather phenomenon easier than ever, with meteorologists giving more advanced forecasts and timely bad weather warnings, as often as not. The amount of data that computers integrate and store in arriving at weather forecasts is now very considerable.

A meteorological discovery appears to have taken place almost 115 years ago that very few people seem to realize even exists. How that discovery was handled at the time, and to this day, is what dissatisfies me with the scientific community at present, at least since the television show about the 4.4 million year old hominid fossil unearthed in the highlands of Ethiopia. That is what I've felt compelled to write about. That a discovery was made, yet is not in encyclopedia, isn't supposed to happen; the discoverer mentions the discovery to someone else, or obtains a patent, and in time the whole world finds out. Why that hasn't happened is open to speculation. 115 years ago, one could argue meteorology was still in its infancy.

There are also things to be observed in cosmology and astrophysics that are curiously missing from any other accounts in those sciences. Neither of those two scientific disciplines are anything like chemistry, where the typical scientist is seen experimenting in a laboratory with ingredients in glass beakers. Cosmologists have little to do, but think about the cosmos. They have no specimens to work with other than astronomical observations, so anyone can read about and observe what is known in the field.

Meteorology also deals with things differently than a laboratory chemist. They don't examine specimens. There aren't specimens to examine other than weather patterns, and radar displays. There are specimens, the weather as it occurs. These are transient phenomena, here one day, gone the next. They aren't things that can be removed from their natural location and examined, though a hail specimen could qualify in that regard. What hail consists of is already known, however, so studying more hail specimens isn't likely to yield much else. Weather phenomenon are things taking place involving huge numbers of gases blanketing the entire planet. Single gas atoms are invisible, but in enormous numbers can gather into weather systems as large as hurricanes. Meteorology is the application of the laws of physics and chemistry to the study of the atmosphere above our planet.

Therefore, anyone with an education, or the ability to read, is able to think about weather phenomena, or cosmology, and perhaps observe something new. Individual components are not so much studied as the aggregate behavior of all air molecules to try to discern what mechanisms drive the weather. The Earth's magnetic field, the jet stream, and the oceans and tides are other huge aggregates that have an impact on the aggregates of the atmosphere.

My objective in writing about this is gaining the attention of the world about all that is written, and gaining enough support to persuade the scientific community to give the process theorized a more accurate and detailed analysis in hopes the theory will emerge as truth. Once that is done, if indeed the truth is found to fit the theory, one should in time be able to look up "Weather Modification" in Encyclopedia and actually find it there.

I would also like to live in a more habitable world. The two events are interconnected. Living conditions won't get better if a process exists that could create perfect growing conditions, little damaging weather, and higher polar ice caps, and encyclopedia don't have it. If the processes I present in this book really work, about the only way for people to find out about it, short of reading this book, would be to find it in an encyclopedia. Once the encyclopedia have it, the world would start becoming a better place.

The theories brought forth here, if eventually proven true, could present the entire population of the world with a new alternative to passively accepting whatever weather comes along, good or bad. The local residents of an area changes at national boundaries, and with weather systems being a natural event that respects no human boundaries, there are sure to be overlapping effects that would spill over to adjacent areas. Anyone who reads this should see the necessity of having all the details described put into perspective, since any attempt to modify the weather, at least from the viewpoint of the theory, would be a local event, confined to a few hundred square miles.

A person living 300 miles from a current drought situation isn't the person strategically located to change weather conditions, should that be deemed necessary. Neither is that person impacted much by the drought 300 miles away, except maybe by rising prices for some foods. The world would become a better place by having the processes described here available to the public since whenever a drought arose some child living in the area would look up weather modification in some encyclopedia and find that there is indeed a solution to the problem included therein. More likely, if these processes do make the encyclopedia, some group of persons everywhere would be entrusted with seeing that drought doesn't develop, or flooding occur. As with any knowledge held by the human species, not all humanity will know this; the grand sum of human knowledge is never held by any one individual, we all hold differing bits and pieces of the total. That is the reason for record keeping of any kind in the first place. An encyclopedia contains the stored wisdom of the species, and when a question arises pertaining to a certain field, the first place to start is often the encyclopedia. The mortise and tenon arrangement used to fasten pieces of furniture together was developed once. It didn't need to be worked out again since it was a part of recorded knowledge, found in encyclopedia.

It may have taken a while from the first practice of that type of carpentry to the final placement of the technique in an encyclopedia, but that is usual for any new idea, method, or process. Currently, if I want to build a chair, I don't have to start from scratch and figure out how to fasten it together by myself. I can look it up in an encyclopedia, or read a book about carpentry. The same conditions apply to just about any field of endeavor and the stored knowledge in that field.

Scientists should be precise and honest about what has been discovered. If the scientific world doesn't follow up and confirm the validity of an idea or process, it has no chance. There should not be any political motivation to fail to mention things that have been discovered, after some time has passed and there are no existing patents. Scientists often work on proprietary material of some corporation that has expended time and assets in the acquisition of this or that process. I don't see a problem with scientists withholding information in the interests of the corporation they work for. It seems a long time has passed with regards to the first time anyone noticed things pertaining to what this book is basically about. There will be no patent for a process that has been around for almost 115 years, if I or anyone else were to apply for it.

Not all scientific inquiry is private. Many colleges and universities have scientific investigations, along with charitable institutions, and information is shared publicly, if something new is discovered. These institutions are dedicated to the pursuit of truth; I can't understand why some of the scientists or future scientists in this group haven't resolved the issues raised in this book long ago. A precedent was set long ago that made any investigation of the processes we will look at difficult for a student to pursue. Professors discouraged students from trying to pursue such a topic for a thesis, following the precedent, and suggested some other topic.

The first chapter will start with some discussion about weather in general. From there it is on to the start of the theory, and a start on explaining it. The next two chapters are the cosmological parts of the book. That cosmological discoveries could have an impact on meteorology is one of the main points of this book; the dynamics of the weather is what man seeks to know. If those dynamics are changed when one factors in huge quantities of as yet undetected particles, we should know that also. How tiny things behave in space can be answered correctly only if we know whether space is a fabric of some kind, or an increate void, composed of empty coordinates through which matter and energy pass.

The fourth chapter discusses the meteorological aspects of the process the author purports to solve all problems in the weather arena. Certainly there are other more urgent problems, most notably pollution, which dilution with water may even exacerbate or only after very long periods of time remedy, and then only if the polluting has stopped. These other problems seem outside the scope of this book. The worst case scenario, the "Mad Max" type of world where there is no flowing water anywhere seems the type of environment current society seems intent upon. That way, no pollutants seep anywhere, and all land masses are deserts, hopefully with desalinization plants. Obviously such an ecosystem would not allow for very many living organisms, and be doomed to failure. Movies without any flowing water anywhere have been on the increase, yet the process we will get to would render that type of dry environment unrealistic and very unlikely.

The fifth chapter is a bit of discussion about this whole concept in general and the impact it might have on the general public of the entire world. Then we get to some of the benefits of these new devices or processes and the costs of letting this slip through our fingers in Chapter 6. Chapter 7 takes a look ahead, and tries to explain what might follow should civilization adopt a more modern view of weather modification.

Chapter 8 gives some anecdotal evidence, after that are appendix chapters. Chapter 9 takes a look back to when I realized for the first time that weather modification was likely possible and is here for the sake of completeness.

The last chapter consists of suppositions and predictions that should be included, also as a kind of reference. After all, time marches on. Anyone who proposes a new theory in the natural sciences will give details and predictions of the theory. Will a theory stand the test of time, is the question. Only by making predictions and seeing those borne out can the theory stand where others have fallen. My reading in the field of cosmology is limited, and if some of the theories I present have been covered already by a previous author, it wouldn't surprise me. What to me is inevitable should seem to be just as inevitable to anyone else. If indeed that is the case, sincere apologies to whoever may have written about the same observations I have made well in advance of me.

I should also note that scientific inquiry has provided a very significant number of contributions that the author has put to use in theorizing about things, and this book would have been impossible without them. That science is well conducted for the most part is not contested here. There is just one meteorological process science seems to have passed up, and it involves cosmological theory to some extent. My profuse thanks to the scientists who have worked diligently over the years in procuring bits of information. All new information is staggering, and sorting through existing theories and new developments, along with established findings has probably left me in a position where I have bitten off more than I can chew.

I am convinced there is something to all that is discussed that isn't immediately apparent. A fair number of findings in the natural sciences involve discoveries that are tried and true but are quite invisible to the naked eye, as in the case of the force of gravity. We know it is there, but there is no putting one's finger on it. You can't point to it and say "this is gravity", or for that matter, any of the forces of nature. They exist, and are surely at work, but their workings are only induced after long and patient observation, and take quite considerable explaining.

Explaining gravity by jumping, and pointing out gravity brought the jump to a quick end does explain gravity, in the sense that one can perceive that gravity is surely at work and the huge mass of the Earth was surely responsible for the jump ending so quickly. But that doesn't explain it entirely, for we have yet to discern what the total particles of the Earth are actually doing to attract things towards them, and then be able to depict one single hydrogen atom, and its singular activity with regard to gravity. For each single atom has some kind of activity it conducts in regards to gravity, which is now only understood by seeing this activity in huge things such as the Earth.

Black holes are known to exist, though no one has ever visited one nor is anyone likely to. They cannot be seen. They can be inferred to exist because of the blank space at the center of the Milky Way, the gravitational effects seen there,the vanishing star in that region of space, and other evidence. Dark Matter and Dark Energy are even more enigmatic than black holes and the forces of nature. But, scientists have enough evidence to induce that Dark Matter and Energy exist, as well.

Dark matter, dark energy, and black holes are real things, surely. Processes involving various things interacting with other things are not tangible things themselves, but nevertheless these processes exist and can eventually be discerned. A weather process unknown to this point, at least so far as not being found in encyclopedia, can be proven to exist. Once discovered, humans should then treat it in the same manner as any new process. In this instance, Weather Modification is the topic where it should be located.

Any new process will be treated with suspicion, and this one could be dangerous, so let the reader decide. My education goes no further than a two year degree in accounting, with no scientific background. Surely, more clever beings exist than myself, having spent six years or more studying meteorology. I am not the first and only person to have perceived something pertaining to weather modification that no one else ever has. The 1957 novel by Ayn Rand, Atlas Shrugged, may have pertained to what this book is about. Ayn Rand passed away in 1982. Some definite similarities exist between the process described herein and what the invention in that novel consisted of, an invention withheld from the world.

Facing weather inevitability head on with as much information as possible seems the best approach. My writing this book clearly shows that adopting an ostrich type of view to these processes isn't working. More individuals besides myself have noticed the same things that more and more people will discover eventually. Humans need this issue successfully resolved, and soon.

The weather may be the most discussed topic on the planet. Most of that discussion is part of the culture of many societies when greeting someone. “Hello, looks like a nice day today” is superficial talk about the weather. Here we go deeper. Some parts of the book diverge from meteorology, and these differing theories are intriguing possibilities, when one views cosmology, life in general, and the entire cycle of the Earth’s ecosphere, as we review all that pertains.

Chapter 1.Background and Theory

Just sitting there it is a Machine

JB

Weather modification in the manner written upon here involves electrical conductivity and resistance, and how these electrical processes could do things to the weather. We will assume throughout this book that just about everyone agrees that experiencing pleasant, livable, yet occasional rainy weather is favored over weather that could endanger lives. The objective of any effort to modify the weather ought to have as its purposes making weather less dangerous, and to make fresh water available worldwide. Almost daily around the globe, some weather extremity can be found to be happening that everyone in the area would rather not have happening.

There are currently a number of land areas that are classified as deserts, and some semi-arid places as well, places that could always use more water. The largest is the Sahara Desert, about 6 million square miles, and some islands have desert on one side, some of the smallest deserts. Every time a flood occurs, that water might have been sent elsewhere, to any one of the dry areas of Earth, had the local residents of the dry areas known they could have as much precipitation as they like. Correspondingly less would occur in any one local area if the entire world is intent upon obtaining an ample supply of water. Splendid results appear inevitable If weather modification was determined to be possible. The idea would be to decentralize all the moisture that is always evaporating from the oceans, and also to get precipitation to fall where it is desired. If the total of water vapor over the entire Earth were viewed as a large hose of incredible power, the idea would be to cut slits in the hose in various places so that all the water doesn't wind up in one place, but was more widely distributed around Earth.

That we have a blanket of atmospheric entities covering the planet that can become way too numerous in any one location is evident. Something with which to modify atmospheric quantities seems the thing really needed. Reducing humidity in one location by increasing humidity in twelve different locations in the same hemisphere could not only stop the imminent flooding in the one location, it would also serve to increase precipitation amounts in twelve other arid regions. If such a process exists that would definitely seem the best alternative.

The stance of the meteorological community concerning modifying the weather is that it isn't possible. Apart from limited success with silver iodide cloud seeding, which raises cloud yields some 30% or thereabouts, no real means of modifying the weather exists. A research project involving electromagnetic pulse propagation, the High Altitude Auroral Research Program, or HAARP for short, is expected to eventually do things with the weather, but officially, not yet.

The Soviets have a complementary version of HAARP, called Woodpecker. There are accusations on the internet that the Russians use the equipment they have to create high pressure in the middle of the Pacific, leading to drought for the western U.S., as the westerlies flow from the Pacific Ocean to the western coast of the U.S. Chem-trails, exhaust from airplanes with special additives, has been tried also. That would be a silver iodide cloud seeding type of experiment. Accusations have been levied against the Canadian government on the internet for conducting such activity and not telling the public about it.

There have been some articles written recently that point to the reluctance of meteorologists to share new information in the field of meteorology. These mostly involve electromagnetic pulse technology and the ignorance of the public when it comes to knowledge of what HAARP is up to. The official position is that HAARP is not currently doing anything with the weather, but there are some voices that say otherwise.

As for what one could hope to achieve if weather could be modified by human activity, growing more and healthier plants and animals on a worldwide basis would be one benefit. No humans starving to death would be a big plus. Never seeing water shortages or famine, knowing when it will rain with certainty gives one a sense of well-being that would be hard to measure in monetary terms. Putting out forest fires with the new technology would also save lives and property. Making shipping lanes safer for ocean going ships, any craft on the open sea, is also a possibility.

The absence of cyclones, tornadoes, and floods would bring an end to the rebuilding of structures destroyed by weather, allowing more buildings to stand for hundreds of years. More precipitation in the polar regions could help to build higher ice caps, and additionally drain the oceans of the strength to generate hurricanes, typhoons, or cyclones. Doesn't seem there is really a choice for mankind should the magic wand be found that humanity could modify the weather with. We have yet to reach the end of the benefits that weather control could provide, we will get to a few more later, and it seems from this point on that doing nothing with the technology, if it existed, would be a lot more dangerous than embracing it.

The atmosphere on our planet contains vast quantities of individual, extremely tiny things. The smallness of these free floating gases is nearly impossible to grasp. That is what meteorology investigates. Also, astrophysicists, cosmologists and others are now claiming that as much as 96% of all matter and energy is dark. A search has been mounted for dark matter and dark energy.

This implies not only is the atmosphere comprised of tiny gases and a little dust, it is also comprised of particles even smaller in amounts as high as up to twenty four times the mass and energy of the atmosphere itself. Meteorology can be a bit more complicated when one considers all possibilities.

There is something to be discovered involving electrical conductivity and resistance and weather modification. The first evidence of this appears with the experiments conducted by Nikola Tesla in 1899, in Colorado Springs, Colorado with his Tesla Coils. A book about Tesla[1] mentions that during the time he was experimenting at Colorado Springs with his Tesla Coils on the platform above his laboratory an intense thunderstorm with some 12,000 lightning bolts in a two hour period occurred once, all the lightning occurring within 30 miles of Tesla's lab.

The biography mentions that thunderstorms in the mountains are a common event in that area of Colorado, not far from Pike's Peak. It is likely that the second half of 1899 saw a higher than average rainfall amount in Colorado Springs, and nearby areas. The presence of a large quantity of copper in a high place such as the Tesla Coils in Colorado Springs was the catalyst for the storm fronts that developed, by being large enough to create a path of least resistance for all air bound entities to flow more freely along.

Tesla tinkering with wireless experiments showed to anyone who happened to be watching a new discovery that should have exploded onto the newspapers after a few weeks; that a large quantity of copper placed strategically could change the weather. Communications being primitive at this time, something Tesla was trying to improve, it could have taken some time for a newsworthy item to traverse the globe, and with this discovery that apparently never happened. The electricity that Tesla pumped into the air found clouds to reside in and from there it was released as lightning. The clouds were probably there because the copper was where it was. To suppose that no one noticed that the Tesla coils were causing any changes to the weather then would be a serious mistake.

The magic wand was seen for the first time, and proved to be rather too large for any one person to wield. The device is just a quarter to half ton of copper, elevated to the highest area around, using whatever labor and equipment. Copper is the cheapest metal with high conductivity. No matter whether trucks and forklifts or manual labor are used to transport it, a quantity of copper placed in a high location is our “magic wand”. Something besides magic is at work when copper in quantities meets the atmosphere.

Exactly what takes place when such a placement of copper on high occurs is the question this book attempts to answer more thoroughly. One notices, also, that the electrical flow could have been reversed, and, instead of sending electrical current skyward, Tesla could possibly have sat patiently and collected electricity from lightning.

These were the first experiments we know with copper in quantity placed on high. Tesla's ideas about controlling the weather could pertain to this, ideas of his that he never developed. From accounts of his trip to Colorado Springs his Tesla coils resided on the roof of his laboratory from early June 1899 until January 1900 when he returned to New York.

Actual 1899 photo

Here is part of the same biography of Tesla; [2] "At dusk of that day Tesla had watched a dense mass of strongly charged clouds gathering in the west. Soon the usual violent storm broke loose which after spending much of its fury in the mountains, was driven away at great speed over the plains". The author states that he felt he had made a great discovery that day; He summed up the import of this discovery thus: "Impossible as it seemed, this planet, despite its vast extent, behaved like a conductor of limited dimensions. The tremendous significance of this fact in the transmission of energy by my system had already become quite clear to me. Not only was it practicable to send telegraphic messages to any distance without wires, as I recognized long ago, but also to impress upon the entire globe the faint modulations of the human voice, far more still, to transmit power, in unlimited amounts to any terrestrial distance and almost without loss". He felt he discovered how to transmit power cheaply that day, as well as send the human voice around the globe. I expected to see something about weather modification then but it wasn't there.

Another part does mention weather modification; "I am positive in my conviction that we can erect a plant of proper design in an arid region, work it according to certain observations and rules, and by its means draw from the ocean unlimited amounts of water for irrigation and power purposes. If I do not live to carry it out, somebody else will, but I feel sure that I am right". The author states "This idea too went into his legacy of unfinished business, and to this day no one has implemented it"[2].

Getting back to those two sentences about the usual violent storm, the whole time that the Tesla Coils were in Colorado Springs, from mid-June of 1899 or before to January 1900, there probably was not one consecutive week where no storms at all occurred, and were more like twice a week, and oft times during the warm months in the mountains during periods of low pressure, storms can threaten in the early to mid afternoon every day for weeks on end. All summer long, then, and into early fall, storms probably threatened nearly every day, with an occasional break when a cold front followed a storm front, followed by new storm development.

Mountainous terrain is indeed quite a different situation than rolling hills or flat prairies. As the winds from the prevailing westerlies reach the base of a mountain, the air will begin to rise, especially during the hours of most intense sunlight. As the air rises it cools, and in so doing, any water vapor in the rising air condenses into clouds. When there is lower pressure and more humidity, those clouds can become thunderstorms very easily and quickly, blossoming in a few short hours.

Florida has frequent thunderstorms for an entirely different reason, since it is one of the flattest states, topographically. The warm waters of the Gulf of Mexico create huge amounts of water vapor that pass right over Florida almost continuously. The high humidity and rising air in Florida during the hours of most intense sun causes the water vapor to rise and condense as well, and since there is a lot of moisture and sunlight is more direct, storms occur rapidly and intensely often.

In Colorado Springs in 1899, once the seasons changed and temperatures fell, the storms would most likely have become less frequent, down to around two per week. That was the discovery, and in the Colorado Springs newspaper from that time the truth could be ascertained as to the frequency of storms in the area for that six or seven month period, and so the list of evidence grows, maybe. I have heard that 1899 set records in respect to rain in that year, but still haven't seen proof.

Finding the exact causes for what happens with

a large quantity of copper on a mountainside could take considerable doing. The assertion maintained to be true throughout this book will be that observable effects can be noted; these are falling barometric pressure, cloud accumulation, and precipitation, the latter usually occurring about 72 hours after placement. The experiments I tried were limited, and there would surely be variation at other locations. One would have to begin at some specific place and perceive what effects occurred there using varying amounts of copper.

One important thing to realize, though, is no location on Earth is isolated from the rest of the Earth in the atmospheric sense. The atmosphere on the planet is interconnected. If some atmospheric gasses begin to move faster eastward, others fill the space that has been vacated by those. If there is lower barometric pressure found along a narrow corridor, higher pressure outside that area would squeeze the lower pressure area, intensifying the effect. It is probable that almost any location will see effects from placing copper strategically, one need only ascertain the effects at some specific location, and decide the appropriate quantity of copper to use so as to yield the desired sized storm.

Not all land areas on earth are mountainous. This should not prove to be an insurmountable problem when it comes to finding a suitable location to place copper where it is one of the highest things around, and be capable of sending electromagnetic waves a long distance. In places such as the Midwestern United States where there are only gentle hills for miles on end, the roofs of tall buildings would probably be a good place to position the copper high enough to produce the desired effects.

Solid objects would block any electromagnetic waves considerably, and decrease the effective range and strength of the waves, so there is the requirement that these copper placements be in an elevated location, with as few land objects above them as possible. One would have to factor in the likelihood of lightning striking the copper, so the rooftop method has a little danger involved. The highest point in a four county area could be found, and a place set aside there.

What happened in Colorado Springs didn't go unnoticed; more tests were conducted by persons unknown, resulting in the three decades of wet weather in the United States from 1900 to 1930. The decade from 1930 to 1940 is known as the Dust Bowl era, a time when the experimenters changed the experiment from utilizing copper, causing precipitation, to lead, which would have the opposite effect of copper, and tend to cause barometric pressure to rise, and inhibit clouds.

This dry period didn't last an entire decade by historical accounts. I looked up the Dust Bowl, and the worst years were 1930 to 1936. Some areas still continued to suffer from drought all the way up to 1940 before weather patterns changed and the great plains saw more precipitation again. Oklahoma, Texas, and all the way into Canada experienced drought during that decade.

The first year of the Dust Bowl was 1930, no rain for a semiarid place to begin with, the Great Plains. The poor farming practices of the three previous decades, when rain was abundant, left the soil exposed, and there were black sky windstorms as drought set in. The topsoil blew away in the wind. There are now rows of trees as windbreaks planted throughout much of the farmland in the U.S.

That wet period during the first three decades of the 20th century saw the Mississippi River overflow its banks 5 or 6 times. The Great Mississippi Flood of 1927 was the most significant of the flooding that occurred. Prohibition brought stills to Appalachia. Each still would have a few good lengths of copper refrigerator tubing for condensation coils, a part of the alcohol creating process. They were usually hidden on hillsides of dense forest, so they were located high up. The end of prohibition didn't happen until 1933, when Roosevelt signed legislation legalizing some alcoholic beverages. That means whiskey stills were still scattered around Appalachia for three years or more after the Dust Bowl began.

The wet weather of those three decades began before prohibition brought moonshine, but then, who really knows how long bootleg whiskey was getting made in such a sparsely populated and densely forested region. Could be that bootleg whiskey reached its height at the time of the worst flooding, and condensation coils from whiskey stills were the cause of problems of too much rain in the middle of the country in the first place. The middle of the United States was wet back then, but the desert southwest remained desert like. The stock market crashed in 1929. The Dust Bowl followed the next spring. The stock market crashed due to unlimited credit expansion, and the Dust Bowl probably began because somebody decided to cash in on the stock market crash and exacerbate the problem with drought, selling short the whole while.

If a human agency was responsible for the wet weather, it follows that the same agency could have seen a strategic opportunity to profit from the stock market crash. Short selling may not have been possible back then, I don't know the date of the stock market permitting short sales. It may have been one reason for the Great Depression in the first place. What I do know is unlimited credit was the norm, but it may have been limited to buying on margin. Nevertheless, patience would have rewarded any human agency with wealth to buy stocks at lows in 1933 or thereabouts.

A foreign country could have done something as this to strengthen the position of its own country in worldwide trade. The drought began right after the stock market crash, the very next spring. Appalachia isn't very far from the Mississippi river, but it is a bit distant from the Great Plains; two agencies are involved in causing the repeated flooding of the great river, but only one agency, somewhere west of the Mississippi, caused wet weather to begin and end in the Great Plains.

As to how one can precisely pinpoint a cause and effect relationship between copper, or lead on a mountain or other high location and specific weather events, proof would only be inferred if experiments did confirm the same, or in weather events, a similar result, in each instance. The evidence would need to rule out coincidence. That just applies to ascertaining that changes are caused by the inserted metal in a high location; it leaves unanswered what combination of many possible causative factors bring about the change.

Obviously the presence of the copper is causing lower barometric pressure, clouds, and rain. The why of that is complicated by the electromagnetic force of the copper, much more powerful than the gravitational force, the conductivity of the copper and the effective range of the electromagnetic waves emanating from them, the size of the copper placement compared to the size of all atmospheric components, and quite a few other factors. This event maintained to be inevitable could involve the water molecules being responsive to electrical fields, the Earth's magnetic field, the jet stream, particles of dark matter and dark energy being charged, whatever static electricity might be doing, and even the propensity of hydrogen atoms to form weak molecular bonds with anything they meet.

There are, no doubt, obscure meteorological journals that have something on this subject in some past archive. My inability to find much about the subject doesn't mean it doesn't exist. An archived article about this subject that dismisses what is asserted here, written prior to 1980, would not convince me, and the overall efficiency of science in general is suspect if some such articles exist. The proof is in the pudding, more clouds.

For successful weather control, cooperation on a global scale would be needed, and that might not be an insurmountable problem either. It could be this discovery will be the catalyst for a change of attitude on the part of a number of people toward other members of the species. If a problem needs to be resolved and the solution involves the cooperation of the entire world, such an activity might help to form more comfortable relations between all the peoples of the world, a likely event when abundance and fewer disasters would likely be the result worldwide.

There is friendly competition between nations, and that could extend to a gardening competition. A contest that would depend on optimal weather for the victor to claim the prize could begin, where judges oversee and ascertain the condition of uncultivated wildlife. No use of hoses or other irrigation devices are allowed but these processes discussed here, and each participating country trying to win the prize acting together achieves the worldwide goal of distributing water safely and plentifully to all land areas. Less would be left to the oceans to create hurricane type activity.

Island chains eventually look after themselves, whenever the need arises, for arranging some precipitation. On some of the resort islands where the lifestyle is more laid back, some of the residents may begin toying with making clouds. Clouds would come easily on islands. Different quantities of copper in varying locations on islands produce different clouds, and lead would make the clouds vanish in varying ways depending on where it is. When thunder and lightning is occurring, fireworks could be added to the event, making island thunderstorms that much more spectacular.

Island cloud makers could even become adept at making clouds appear to resemble objects roughly, at least for a short while, and as the years progress, island life changes to accommodate the new sport of cloud making as an art. Sun bathing tourists get a free art display in the sky, clouds disappearing completely at times followed by some unusually shaped clouds, clouds suddenly appearing on one side of an island and then vanishing as they cross to the other side, etc. The cloud view could be an added feature on resort islands in the future.

Water is precious, but it is also present in very large quantities. The only problem facing man is how to distribute the water over the land masses of the planet. Placing copper tubing in a high location at strategic times could so cheaply redistribute fresh water around the planet and prevent extreme weather from destroying things, provided the entire world is intent upon an ample supply of water, that it is important that not much further time be wasted taking this idea forward.

The atmosphere is made of mostly electrically neutral particles, that are unaffected by the copper, leaving only the gravitational force to influence the atmosphere, a force that is 100 billion times weaker than the electromagnetic force. The stable isotopes of nitrogen and oxygen, N_2, and O_2, are neutral electrically and that is 99% of the known air, and most of the remaining one percent is also neutral. A path of least resistance created by a quantity of copper placed in a high location won't at first glance seem likely to have much of an effect on the atmosphere, or weather.

The water molecule is not electrically neutral. It is a polar molecule. A book, "Giant Molecules; Here, There, And Everywhere", by Alexander Yu. Grosberg and Alexei R. Khokhlov on page 43, 44 and 45 discusses the nature of water. Some of what was written follows; “The water molecule is triangular in shape. The electron cloud tends to be shifted away from the hydrogen nuclei toward the oxygen nucleus by, on average (a certain amount in an equation). As a result, the positive charge of the hydrogen nuclei is not quite compensated. Similarly, there is an uncompensated negative charge around the oxygen nucleus. This peculiarity of the structure may not seem of great significance at first sight. However, it is the real cause of all the special properties of water that make it play such an important role in living organisms. A water molecule has a considerable dipole moment, so the molecule is polar. This means that in an external electrical field water molecules can be regarded as little "dipoles," each carrying two charges, +E and -E, separated by a distance. Such little dipoles have no difficulty in becoming aligned in an external electrical field; this explains why the dielectric permeability of water is much higher than for all other common liquids."[3]

The statement about alignment in an external electrical field is referring to water in liquid form in a container. All water molecules in the container would have the hydrogen atoms pointing one way, and the oxygen atoms the other, when exposed to an external electrical field, provided the water is sitting still in the container. Those observations lead to the observation that water molecules in gaseous form would react to an external electrical field such as the Tesla Coils on the roof of his laboratory in Colorado Springs during the second half of 1899, as it orbited the planet.

Since water molecules are very weak magnets, using a huge magnet similar to what junk yards use to lift junk cars by placing it high up and activating the electrical current might do an even more efficient job of herding water molecules to a desired location. A utility company could have a little fenced off area near a mountaintop with a small generator connected to a huge magnet there. When precipitation is required, someone activates the generator, providing the magnet with electrical current. After desired precipitation quantities are reached, the generator is turned off, and the magnet is not pulling water molecules toward it.

Reverse the direction of the current, and the ensuing negative charge will repel the negatively charged oxygen nucleus of each water molecule. Since the oxygen nucleus in a water molecule is larger by far than the two hydrogen nuclei, those two hydrogen nuclei are always along for the ride, the larger component deciding where the molecule travels. Thus, positive or negative charges from a huge electromagnet in a high location could mimic purified copper or lead deposits similarly located. Proof would still be required to satisfy scientific rigor. Now there is more than one mechanism to be tested. A path of least resistance might not be necessary with the use of huge magnets instead

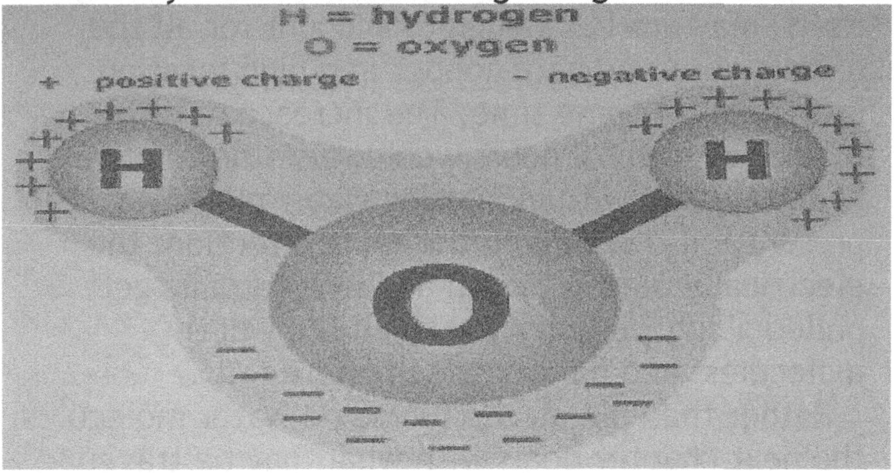

The larger oxygen nucleus decides the path of the water molecule

of copper in the hundreds of pounds. That remains to be established as well. Nevertheless, the passive placement of a large quantity of copper located in a strategic position to alter atmospheric components is by far a less expensive alternative to electromagnets, which would require the expenditure of electric current, an expense in the electrical accounting of things, rather than the expected benefit of catching lightning and reaping millions of volts of electricity.

A placement of copper tubing in a row in a high location, propagating electromagnetic waves at the speed of light, spread out over a hundred feet or so, weighing 500lbs., is so large in relation to the size of individual atmospheric components that there is little doubt that anything not electrically neutral would be influenced by it considerably. The size difference is definitely one factor, making the passive presence of something that conductive and large the workings of a crude machine. It would do the same thing an electromagnet would do without wasting energy.

Water vapor varies at any one location, and by itself, may not be enough to account for all the effects observed with copper in a high location left there for some time. The increase of water molecules over 72 hours would raise the relative humidity, and with increasing water molecules present, all traveling in the same direction, the electrically inert nitrogen and oxygen pairs get pulled along via gravity with all the water molecules, and barometric pressure falls.

Rather than pin all the blame on water molecules, the next chapter deals with what may be traveling with water molecules along the path of least resistance. The scientific community doesn't think the properties of the water molecule itself to be significant enough to cause changes in the weather, since this process isn't already in encyclopedia.

There really isn't that much water by weight in the air when the saturation point is reached. 100% relative humidity at 30C is 3% of the atmosphere by weight. Naturally precipitation counts as more than 100% relative humidity, though there is no scale above 100%. Once many water molecules gather together, it is then a raindrop and falling, water molecules no longer suspended in the atmosphere. The usual 99% of the known air, nitrogen and oxygen paired isotopes, can fall to 96% of the known air with relative humidity at its height at this temperature. Some places in the tropics have as much as 5% of the atmosphere comprised of water during storms. For barometric pressure to fall, and all air bound entities to travel in the same general direction, more than just the water molecules are herding along the path of least resistance. These additional entities add more weight to the water molecules following the path of least resistance, those water molecules not comprising sufficient mass by themselves to bring the electrically inert paired isotopes of nitrogen and oxygen along by gravity.

Chapter 2. A Cosmological Explanation

From whence hydrogen, but from parents

JB

There is the likelihood that whatever fragments the Big Bang created have all been condensing into hydrogen atoms all these billions of years and may still exist, comprising the missing energy and mass scientists have been searching for. The smallest thing in the universe, the most abundant thing in the universe also, combines to create hydrogen atoms through a process that will be elaborated upon. Current theories maintain that hydrogen just spontaneously developed early in the history of the known universe and has long ceased.

I see a plastic bag! I see a plastic bag!

Those theories reduce all dark matter and dark energy in the universe to flotsam, junk, debris. Plastic bags in the ocean. Except that the amount of plastic bags far exceeds the oceans. It also points to the universe being grossly inefficient at changing from one thing to another, if only four percent of all existing ever becomes anything detectable.

In the depths of space there are no processes ongoing that would degrade or change whatever fragments that were created in the Big Bang. No bacteria, no oxidization, no erosion, no friction to speak of for something that is individually so small, so the tiny entities that make up the local dark matter and dark energy could still be the same as they were over 13 billion years ago.

The long cooled plasma from the Big Bang still persists, the fragments unable to reduce to any smaller thing. Dark matter and dark energy have thus far not become hydrogen. Hydrogen is the thing we detect in greatest abundance, and is the simplest element with the least number of parts. There must be some unseen event going on that turns dark matter and dark energy into hydrogen, a process that began as soon as the plasma of the Big Bang cooled, and continues today, and will for billions of years in the future.

Dark matter and dark energy are theorized since the known universe is expanding at an increasing rate, and given the mass of stellar objects known, there is not enough mass to slow the expansion and bring it to gravitate back upon itself, creating another big bang.

One of the cosmological theories of the past few decades assumes that the universe will go through cycles where the matter and energy is all pulled together, explodes and radiates outwards, then slows down, gravity pulling everything back together again for yet another explosion, so the cycle repeats. That theory assumes the known universe is all existing.

There must be more matter and energy existing that is undetected, according to theorists. New evidence suggests it is not just theory. The orbits of the celestial bodies are taking place at a much higher speed than they would if what is observable were all that existed. Calculations of astronomers indicate that 74% of the universe is dark energy, 22% is dark matter, and the remaining 4% is the matter and energy already known in the universe.

This may seem a little confusing at first since matter and energy are inextricably intertwined, but astronomical calculations do indicate that more mass and energy must be present, and not in the same quantities. One of the first articles about dark matter and dark energy was from as far back as 1932, but it got little attention until recently.

Energy separates from matter when it is released, as in a nuclear fusion event. Energy is released, or is potential energy that could be released from matter. We would assume that the missing energy and mass are in the form of things that are both.

The two things known as matter and energy are arguably two sides of the same coin. Actually distinguishing when something is energy and when it is matter is not exactly easy. Matter is used to describe the gravitational effects, or aspects of something massive. That same something, say, a star, could explode in a supernova and what was matter and energy is now mostly energy, so the coin has now flipped sides, although gravitational waves are still propagating from every atom. In time, a new solar system with asteroids, planets, moons, comets and a smaller star at its core will coalesce, and the coin will have swung back to a less energetic combination of matter and energy.

Energy refers to what is released from matter. During nuclear fusion, in supernovae, energy is released from matter. On the cosmological scale, energy can vary with the different motions of things. The faster something is going, the more energy it has. The greater the energy, the greater the effect of seeming to pull the known universe apart. The elements can vary in how energetic they are. Five pounds of matter at rest has much less energy than five pounds of matter moving at speeds near the speed of light.

If it turns out to be one particle from whence hydrogen originates it would then take the place of hydrogen as the most abundant thing in the known universe, by far. A book by Dan Hopper, "Dark Cosmos: In Search of Our Universe's Missing Mass and Energy"[4] has some interesting parts. When discussing possible candidates for the missing particle the author writes it couldn't be a charged particle, because particles with charge would interact with photons, making them luminous, and thus detectable. That which takes place among particles too small to register on human sensors is unknown. There is a chance that dark matter and dark energy are charged and still go undetected.

An electromagnetic wave coursing through the air from a quantity of nearly pure copper may do something entirely unexpected to particles that small, and they might still remain non-luminous. The search for truth would have to leave room for unexpected possibilities. A particle that is not charged, but behaves like one in the tiny quantum mechanical universe, or a charged one that is so minute that the interactions one would expect it to undergo when encountering a photon are too faint and go undetected couldn't be ruled out.

Magnetic monopoles are thought to have been created by the big bang, as numerous as protons, though it is assumed they would have huge amounts of energy. Some Grand Unified Theories proposed a transition took place in the early Universe, in which the three forces of the Standard Model, the electromagnetic, strong and weak forces emerged from one grand unified force. "As a consequence of this process, an enormous number of strange objects called magnetic monopoles would be generated."[5]

Magnetic monopoles appear to be the thing most likely created in the Big Bang. These are magnetic particles with only one side of a traditional magnet. They are not found in nature in the sense that any magnets discovered or created have always been found to have two poles. This refers to objects large enough for humans to see and touch, and any magnet such as this when cleaved in two, will be two magnets, each a dipole. The magnetic monopoles would be the smallest thing the universe could make, not further reducible, and not contain nearly as much energy as had been speculated.

It is possible each individual magnetic monopole contains a huge amount of energy in comparison to its size, but the particle itself is so small that the energy each contains is also small. If the primordial specks were magnetic monopoles each would be energetic and unstable, a charged particle.

I just doubt that exploded fragments from a huge explosion would be something other than precursors to hydrogen, or other than the smallest thing the universe could possibly make. The primordial soup mentioned on science programs refers to the oceans of the Earth in the early years of its existence. The known universe could be viewed as so much primordial soup early in its existence as well. Hydrogen appears to be the only thing making any progress in the primordial soup of the universe, and much of the universe appears to still be the fragments originally created in the Big Bang, so it seems more likely that hydrogen in the known universe is still on the increase. Things must be changing from one thing to another.

Figures for the distribution of hydrogen in the known universe give us 93% of the known elements, by far the most abundant. Yet that 93% is only 93% of the known matter in the known universe; there is also 96% of the known universe that is dark matter and energy. Distribution of hydrogen on rocky planets like the Earth tails off considerably, the oceans have 11%, 3% in the Earth's crust.

The entire process of hydrogen creation may be a long and still ongoing process. One hydrogen atom by itself is the tiniest atom in existence, and for these to come into existence one at a time, without announcing themselves, we would never be aware of it. Hydrogen always pairs up as stable H_2 isotopes. These hydrogen atoms could be a reproducing pair, in the sense that a spontaneous metamorphosis may occur between the two. The double combination of hydrogen atoms serves as the template. It provides, in the space between the two nuclei, an image into which quantities of primordial specks swarm, somewhat like stem cells. Where they happen to be in the template, they adopt the role of that part of the hydrogen atom. Some contribute to make an electron, most become part of one of the quarks in the nucleus.

The electromagnetic and gravitational waves from the two hydrogen nuclei are very strong forces at such small distances, strong enough to imprint new information onto the primordial specks.

The information transfer complete, a hydrogen atom or a neutron has suddenly come to exist. In the case of neutrons resulting, everything that surrounds the proposed sight of the reproductive event, protons and electrons, are reproduced but housed together; a neutron is a proton and electron bound up together in a nucleus as one thing. Without the nucleus of a nearby element to join and reside in, the proton and electron in a neutron will separate, from 8 to 14 minutes after creation. A neutron is unstable as a stand alone particle. Within other nuclei neutrons can remain stable.

Suppose in a stellar environment with fusion events all around and extreme heat and pressure the newly created offspring is a neutron. In that

No, hydrogen pairs do not make whoopee

kind of environment neutrons would frequently join a hydrogen atom and become part of a deuterium atom and that atom could join another deuterium atom to make helium through nuclear fusion, and the neutrons could join other elements. A neutron is much smaller than a hydrogen atom as a neutron lacks an electron in orbit, and would be even more difficult to detect should one such entity suddenly exist when a moment previously it did not.

Enlarge a paired isotope of hydrogen atoms until the two nuclei are the size of a grain of salt. The space separating the two nuclei would have grown to 200 feet or more, and the electrons would be 100 feet or more away from each nucleus. From that perspective it is evident there is room for tiny particulates. The diameter of the nucleus of a hydrogen atom is 1.75 femtometers. The electron cloud around a hydrogen atom is 145,000 times the size of the nucleus itself. That makes the electron cloud just larger than a quarter of a nanometer.

Enlarge the nucleus one million times, and it is 1.75 nanometers, only visible with a microscope. How big the electron orbital would be once the nucleus reaches the size of a grain of salt would depend on the grain of salt. If the electron orbits in a path 145,000 times bigger than the nucleus, that would mean that the orbital path of the electron is 145,000 grains of salt in diameter.

With 24 grains of salt per inch, the electron would be in orbit in a circle slightly more than 500 feet in diameter. At 40 grains of salt to an inch, the electrons orbital path would be slightly more than 300 feet in diameter. Even 60 grains of salt to an inch, if the other estimates seem low, leaves the electron a hundred feet away from the nucleus, in a path 200 feet in diameter.

A grain of salt in a bubble nothing can penetrate at least 200 feet in diameter. All that space for one grain of salt, with an electron 2840 times smaller circling. Two hydrogen atoms together in a paired isotope with separate nuclei would each have one electron circling, though the electrons would probably switch nuclei and do figure eights simultaneously, with the two electrons traveling so fast and always changing orientation that only a residual cloud is detectable.

Each nucleus would have an electron shield preventing the other from coming any closer. The two nuclei would be a minimum of 200 feet apart, to more than 500 feet apart, with the nuclei the size of grains of salt of various sizes.

A larger atomic nuclei would have one nucleus with many protons and neutrons bound together, with a swarm of electrons buzzing around it. An iron atom would have a nucleus the size of a small pebble were it enlarged like the hydrogen atom, and dozens of electrons circling however many feet away. The nucleus of a uranium atom wouldn't be much bigger, a slightly larger pebble than iron.

It would seem an exaggeration two things small as grains of salt at least 200 feet apart would do anything to smaller things 100 feet away, but it does give us an insight into possible hydrogen reproduction by the stable paired isotope of hydrogen. After all, the real distance between two hydrogen atoms is very small. Taken at its actual size, the electron shield provided by rapidly circling electrons around a pair of hydrogen atoms may very well prove insufficient at preventing everything from entering the area between the

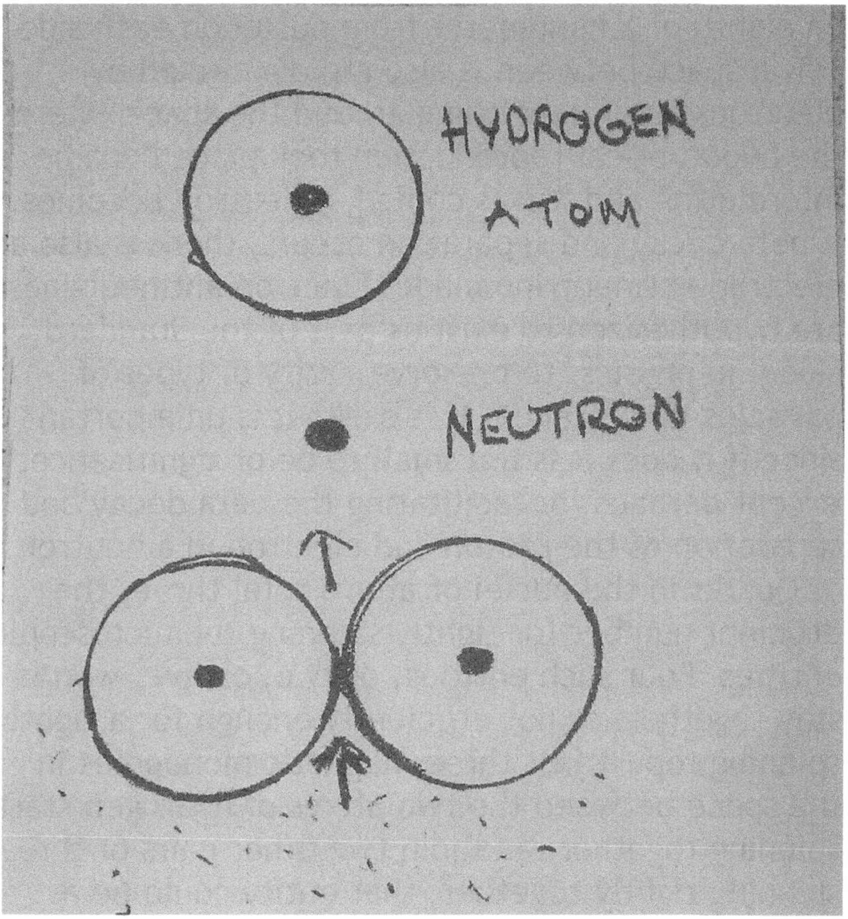

Hydrogen pair in the primordial soup

two nuclei, since hypothetically dark matter and dark energy components could be small enough to enter that space. Two hydrogen atoms, each surrounded by an electron cloud just more than a quarter nanometer in diameter, would be about that far apart from each other, the distance of the radii of the two electrons. Something in the space between the two identical nuclei would be about an eighth of a nanometer from nuclei on each side.

The space between is also rapidly circled by electrons, so if everything around the space where the hypothetical reproduction took place became information and it was copied, a neutron becomes. If beta decay and separation occurs, there is also an electron antineutrino made. Electron antineutrinos are hypothesized to exist as part of the Standard Model in physics, to preserve parity of types of particles in existence. If it exists it is unimportant since if it does it is too small to be of significance, except perhaps for facilitating the beta decay and separation of the proton and electron in a neutron.

Quarks in the nuclei of atoms total three, the efficient number for tightly spinning submicroscopic entities. Four such entities, or two, or five, won't stay together, or not efficiently enough for a tightly spinning top. If just three magnetic monopoles in the space between the two atoms of hydrogen start spinning together, and join two other pairs of three spinning tightly together, that entity could be a third of a quark. Two more such groups of three join that one, and a quark becomes. That happens twice more, and 81 magnetic monopoles make a hydrogen atom nucleus, with a small part of one adopting the role of an electron. It is a simple explanation, but nature is simple. A gear within a gear, within a gear, all spinning tightly, all groups of rapidly circling magnetic monopoles.

It could be the rapidly spinning triplets of matter are even more compiled and stacked upon each other, in which case 243 magnetic monopoles would make a proton, or possibly even 729. 2187 of them makes the magnetic monopoles too impossibly small for words, but one would have to suppose that even that small of a magnetic monopole may exist.

Events happening within a single paired isotope of hydrogen will probably remain impossible to ever actually see. That neutrons are produced within stars is pretty well established. That seems a clear indication hydrogen is created as neutrons in a stellar environment where these neutrons can often combine with the nucleus of a nearby atom and remain part of some element indefinitely, while those that do not unite with another atom decay into a proton, an electron and an electron anti-neutrino, from within 8 to 14 minutes. The absence of much deuterium in the known universe in general doesn't preclude the chance that neutrons are the creation of hydrogen atom pairs.

On Earth, any neutrons created almost always decay into protons, electrons and electron anti-neutrinos, while in stars, neutrons often join hydrogen to become deuterium, and deuterium transitions through fusion eventually into helium. Neutrons are joining other elements as well, like carbon, oxygen, lithium, nitrogen, and whatever other elements that are within the star.

Very few neutrons undergoing beta decay result in the electron and proton being together. They are both thrown out and away from each other, along with the electron antineutrino. A rare kind of decay results in the electron and proton staying together, but very rarely. In the early stages of the known universe when there was nothing but magnetic monopoles and hydrogen that drifted in from afar, whenever beta decay of a newly made neutron took place, the electron all by itself would have nothing to do but be captured by a proton, and the proton would have nothing to do but capture an electron. Before stars coalesced and fusion began to take place, if neutrons were being created by two simple hydrogen atoms, and either underwent beta decay or became deuterium, and no heavier elements were in existence but growing amounts of hydrogen and some deuterium, the end result would inevitably be increasing amounts of hydrogen atoms, which would reproduce more.

The entire process from magnetic monopoles to simple hydrogen has a few more stages, from neutrons to protons and electrons which eventually unite to form simple hydrogen. If neutrons are the product of hydrogen nucleosynthesis through the paired hydrogen isotope, some could join the nucleus of hydrogen atoms, and become deuterium, and remain so until stars formed. Then they would participate in fusion to produce helium.

Chances are some deuterium created in the early years of the known universe lasted billions of years before stars ignited and almost all of it turned into helium through nuclear fusion, and there may have been enough of it for some to become lithium[7], the next step, fusing helium.

It is possible for the same event to occur in the early universe if the reproduced product of two hydrogen atoms were a simple hydrogen atom, and not a neutron. Once enough hydrogen atoms exist, stars begin to form, and the hydrogen compressing the nucleus of the emerging star converts some hydrogen to neutrons, the star ignites in nuclear fusion and builds helium, and possibly some lithium before any supernova occur.

The Standard Model supposes that those three elements, hydrogen, helium, and a little lithium, are all created in 20 minutes after the Big Bang occurred. Then the universe was finished making heavy particles, and all the heavier elements are produced from these 3 elements in further stellar fusion and supernovae. It is a spontaneous event, a transformation based upon falling temperatures and decreasing density, and whatever other conjecture, leaving 96% of the universe flotsam.

One can easily see, however, that those three elements would also be in the same general abundances 5 billion years or so after the Big Bang, if hydrogen reproduced itself all the while at an increasing rate, as neutrons or hydrogen atoms, and nuclear fusion within stars was just starting. What one can't see is what actually happened, humans didn't exist for over 13 billion years after the Big Bang. Stars exist and undergo supernovae, and that is well established. Maybe the age of the things around us needs reconsidering if a process of hydrogen reproducing itself one at a time albeit in ever growing numbers is involved.

Not every star in the early universe ignited at the same moment. The first stars may have gone through a supernova long before the majority ignited for the first time. These events, star formation, are still occurring in the known universe, now mostly stars from previous supernova, though there are still blue giants about, young stars compared to our Sun.

93% of the known matter of stars is hydrogen, and with gravitational forces being much greater in stars than on Earth, primordial specks would be in greater abundance. Hundreds could be at any moment jockeying for position to wind up in the template to become the next hydrogen or neutron, in a huge number of paired hydrogen isotopes.

Hydrogen is a stable atom, the simplest one. The most pulverized thing possible existing after the Big Bang isn't going to know how to combine into one; the plasma of the known universe, once cooled, soon came into contact with H_2 isotopes from somewhere else in the much larger entire universe, and that encounter set the process of hydrogen production in motion by providing a template for the magnetic monopoles to transform into neutrons, or hydrogen atoms. Since then hydrogen production would have increased as more templates emerge over the eons, as new hydrogen atoms pair up.

An electrical current running through a sealed chamber with a million hydrogen atom pairs within to serve as templates could prove that hydrogen is still coming into existence if left sealed for several months or even a year. Examining the contents after some time should see more hydrogen atoms within than previously. The primordial specks would be pulled toward, and accumulate along the electrical field, pass through the walls of the container, meet hydrogen pairs, and produce hydrogen atoms, or neutrons, which would mature into hydrogen, or its parts, in a quarter hour on Earth. The hydrogen or neutrons would be trapped in the container. One would have to try an empty chamber under the same conditions, to see what happens then.

Neutrons, with electrons compressed within the nucleus and not circling some distance away, are only slightly larger than the nucleus of a hydrogen atom, and could pass through the walls of a vacuum chamber, frustrating experiments, for all I know. Or, the neutron may be able to enter nuclei of atoms present in the chamber wall, but there it could be detected if some accumulations occurred.

More hydrogen, or more neutrons in the walls of the container, gives us the capacity to tell which is the reproduced product, between neutrons or hydrogen atoms on Earth. A little of both, neutrons. Neutrons could be becoming and decaying into protons and electrons and be unable to join other nuclei without the heat and pressure of a stellar environment. In that case, no neutrons would be in the container walls, no deuterium is present, protons and electrons would have reunited, and increased amounts of hydrogen would be found. Thus, if only an increase in hydrogen amounts are found, that doesn't conclusively prove that the original product of the two hydrogen atoms wasn't a neutron originally.

The presence of stars and other celestial bodies changes the environment for the hydrogen atoms and the magnetic monopoles; there are now places where there is little hydrogen, and places where there is a lot. After the Big Bang there was likely little else besides dense clouds of magnetic monopoles and an increasing number of hydrogen atoms, and maybe growing amounts of deuterium. Eventually the hydrogen and possibly deuterium clumps together, grows large and dense enough, and ignites in nuclear fusion. The entire body of stars would have lots of hydrogen templates.

The Earth's atmosphere would have as many H_2 isotopes as the relative humidity in an area. Each water molecule is half hydrogen or neutron factory, under some conditions. The centers of rocky planets and moons wouldn't have many templates for hydrogen or neutron production, especially cold ones like Pluto. The lighter elements would have made for the surface long ago, or be molecularly bound to something else.

The likelihood that stars are continually adding hydrogen atoms, or neutrons, while also losing the same items to nuclear fusion explains how stars can continue to burn for billions of years. It takes much longer to exhaust a fuel supply that is constantly renewed. The Earth doesn't undergo nuclear fusion at its core because it isn't dense enough, being much smaller than the Sun. It would have less hydrogen, or neutrons, being created continually. Earth doesn't have the mass necessary for fusion to occur, or for hydrogen to reproduce rapidly. The weaker gravity of the Earth won't bind as many primordial specks as the Sun and other stars.

The Oceans, indeed, all the water on Earth, each water molecule containing the hydrogen template, could be a source of new hydrogen. These new hydrogen atoms that are hypothetically created in the sea would rise to the atmosphere also, while pairing up, most escaping into outer space, some finding an oxygen atom to join on the way up and out. The oceans would be making more water vapor than mere evaporation would account for, so more would accumulate in any one place if experiments with copper in a high location were attempted. There is simply more moisture available than previous estimates.

To better estimate atmospheric events, the totality of water vapor being created by hydrogen templates creating hydrogen or neutrons that become a part of water molecules themselves would be worthwhile knowing. Maybe a computer simulation with an extra two tons of water daily programmed to come to exist could give a more accurate depiction of available water vapor.

We may already know a little about how much hydrogen is getting created in the Oceans. After all, if that type of activity were going on at a very rapid rate, the Earth would already be almost completely covered in water, so the rate that hydrogen is coming into existence in the oceans probably isn't very rapid, unless the rate that H_2 escapes into outer space is very high. That would mean concentrations of primordial specks here on Earth probably isn't high enough for hydrogen to reproduce rapidly.

The Earth gains tons of mass daily, as meteors are vaporized to dust entering the atmosphere. That is where this weight gain comes from, say scientists. This daily gain of mass could be as much as 100 tons. If two tons of that total were newly created water molecules from newly condensed hydrogen, we would not know whether some of the daily weight gain came from there or not. Measurements of the Earth are taken from space, so what bulges and where is indistinct.

If both dust fell on the surface and hydrogen was created within the sea, and became water on contact with an oxygen atom, amounting to two tons of water daily, the Earth would appear slightly larger daily. If the oceans bulge slightly every day, that could be explained by movements in the Earth's crust, underwater volcanoes, dust accumulating, or an increasing amount of water, or a little of each.

Each day adding a ton of new water to the Earth due to reproduction of hydrogen, water being where some of it would end up, would compare to putting a teaspoon of water in a lake with a surface area of a square mile on a daily basis. A gallon of water is 8 pounds, a ton 250 gallons. Even two tons of water, 500 gallons, wouldn't be at all noticed spread over the oceans on a daily basis. Hydrogen has to combine with oxygen to become a water molecule, so 500 gallons of water isn't all new hydrogen adding to the total weight of the Earth. The oxygen that combined with hydrogen would have been present in the atmosphere, but it now adds to the mass of the Earth as surface water.

The nuclear furnaces of stars would be the place where most hydrogen reproduction would be transpiring. That makes examining such an event closely impossible. Stars being larger than Earth, more primordial specks would be gravitationally bound to a star, the density of those being the key factor in the presence of hydrogen. Where gravity is weaker, the density of primordial specks would usually be below the threshold for hydrogen atoms or neutrons to reproduce, or, as in our case, diffuse enough to slow the process down a lot.

Gas giants in our solar system are probably above the threshold even more so than Earth, so one would expect more of that to be happening on Jupiter, continually adding to the gases present, with condensation adding to the land mass. A space journey to one of the gas giants a hundred years from now may be when hydrogen is proven to still be coming to exist in the known universe.

Primordial specks are around or within all objects of mass that are in the universe. Some of these primordial specks may be in deep space, but most would be bound by gravity to something very massive. All celestial bodies would also have some of this huge amount of mass and energy within them, since the smallness of these things would allow them to pass through solid objects. With regard to black holes, the primordial specks would not be around them but within them, and once that happens they are bound by gravity.

On the surface of the Earth, primordial specks would be in great abundance, a veritable blizzard of them. The extent they reach into outer space surrounding the Earth could be hundreds of miles. If this quantity of dark matter and dark energy are magnetic monopoles they would add to the water molecules following the path of least resistance of hypothesized experiments with copper in quantity in a high location. Not only that, they would also accumulate from a much larger area than water molecules and could multiply in quantities within the region involved much faster than the water molecules. Water molecules have a much limited range in the atmosphere in comparison to dark matter and dark energy, whose range would extend into outer space, and to within the Earth.

Since the initial fragments of our proposed hydrogen precursors all contain mass, albeit in a tiny amount, the mass of all the fragments that accumulate along the path of least resistance created by a quantity of copper strategically placed could exceed considerably the mass of currently known air molecules. At the highest estimate of 96% of all matter being dark energy and dark mass, and assuming Earth has around it a proportionate share of primordial specks, and increased concentrations of primordial specks along the path of least resistance increasing the quantity by a factor of two, for example, the dark matter and dark energy accompanying the atmosphere could be as much as 48 times more matter and energy as the known atmosphere.

Therefore, these small entities would affect the known air molecules gravitationally, air molecules that are not charged, and unaffected in any way by the electromagnetic force of the copper. The water molecule is much larger than the primordial specks, so encounters with it could tend to position the neutral nitrogen and oxygen isotopes along the path of least resistance, since there is also the propensity of hydrogen atoms to try to attach themselves to anything they come close to.

The newly formed hydrogen atoms that have begun to coalesce from increased concentrations of primordial specks and water molecules would pair up as stable H_2 isotopes, and rise, being the lightest element, even if now paired up. As newly condensed paired hydrogen atoms rise, the moment one of these meets a free oxygen atom it joins with the oxygen atom and becomes H_2O. Ozone, O_3, is continually created and destroyed as single oxygen atoms are lost or gained in the upper atmosphere by the stable oxygen isotope, O_2. If the two hydrogen atoms together do produce a neutron, there are more steps the neutron must take to become hydrogen atoms before pairing up. Since the neutron hypothetically created by magnetic monopoles entering the space between two hydrogen atoms is a condensed version of everything surrounding the site of reproduction, with the exception of the hypothetical electron antineutrino, it seems most likely the end result.

After beta decay of neutrons in the sea, or along a path of least resistance where accumulations occurred, one would expect that loose protons and electrons in a 200 square mile region, in copious abundance, would unite to form simple hydrogen atoms with little difficulty, and from there find a partner with which to become the paired isotope, rising through the atmosphere all the while. At that point a paired isotope would only need to get in the proximity of a loose oxygen atom in the ozone layer, and it is a water molecule.

Neutron or hydrogen atom, the newly created entity begins to rise from the sea, or is born in the air, and each is a half hour or more from the ozone layer. Hence, after about the same time passes a neutron being reproduced by hydrogen pairs would do everything that a hydrogen atom would do if it were the product of the paired isotope, except for neutrons being able to join the nuclei of nearby atoms, which some may do, though it is unclear if that is possible outside a stellar environment.

Clouds appearing where none were expected would be explained by this theory. The primordial specks probably reach concentrations sufficient to start synthesizing hydrogen atoms or neutrons inside the H_2 in the water molecules more rapidly than the usual slow rate. The new water molecules join clouds from the ozone layer above, while existing water molecules in the atmosphere from hundreds of miles in every direction would begin gathering along the path of least resistance below, and rise to the clouds.

H_2O is lighter than the isotopes of oxygen and nitrogen. Once a gas, single water molecules would be subject to the influences any molecule in the air would. The molecule would rise from the water surface where it evaporated to the height of clouds, while following the easiest path it could take.

There are other possible assisting causes for the effects perceived with copper creating a path of least resistance. The jet stream could change course as a result of a row of copper tubing changing the magnetic field of the Earth to some extent, significantly increasing cloud development in the direction it changed.

It could be that the static electricity following the path of least resistance weighs more heavily than expected. If the copper attracts static electricity to it, there is then correspondingly less static electricity in the air surrounding the copper, and that could make it easier for the electrically neutral particles to flow along, a narrow corridor where the atmosphere has no static electricity.

There is the tendency of hydrogen atoms to try to form weak molecular bonds with anything they come close to. As more and more water molecules accumulate along the path of least resistance, all flowing in the same direction, each time one of the two hydrogen atoms within the triangular water molecule come close to an electrically inert isotope of oxygen or nitrogen, they try to attach themselves to them. Whether that would result in a slight tug of the inert isotopes along the path of least resistance is entirely possible. It would be fun to show a film that illustrates hundreds of water molecules tugging at the nitrogen and oxygen isotopes, turning them in the same direction that everything else is traveling.

Perhaps the real answer for what happens when copper in quantity is placed in a high location is “all of the above”. Each little thing by itself may not be sufficient to cause weather changes alone, but is part of the equation. The combined effect of all the possible causes produces weather changes.

It looks like a large part of the effects observed are due to the polar nature of the water molecule, and all the primordial specks and the huge amount of mass they bring with them along a path of least resistance, in addition to hydrogen that comes to exist from the increased presence of these. If one were to pie diagram the possible causes, I would give the water molecules at least 40% of the pie, the primordial specks 30%, static electricity 15%, the Jet Stream 10%, and 5% to hydrogen trying to bond to other things. The Earth's magnetic field plays a role, but so does the Sun, the oceans, the tides, the rest of the universe, etc.

Everything existing such as it does and being essential to increasing clouds and precipitation does not make them the cause of such events, though without oceans or the Sun, a magnetic field on Earth, and all of the universe, none of what is predicted to happen could occur. The universe, and all the things in it have existed during times of drought as well, at least in the past. What changes when copper is placed on high surely has more to do with the purity of the copper and its ability to send electromagnetic waves at the speed of light over a vast area, the strength of the electromagnetic waves, and the disparity in size between copper in the hundreds of pounds in a hundred foot row, and the size of the components of the atmosphere affected.

It is clear that despite doubts as to the exact causes of increased clouds and precipitation, nevertheless a quarter ton of copper on an 8000 foot mountainside near an ocean left in place for 72 hours would provide evidence all by itself, especially if one chose to begin experiments when no clouds or precipitation were expected in the next few days by meteorological forecasts. Whoever should happen to try that should have an escape route worked out should it become necessary to suspend the experiment in the interest of safety, a quite likely event if one really placed a quarter ton of copper near an ocean in a high place.

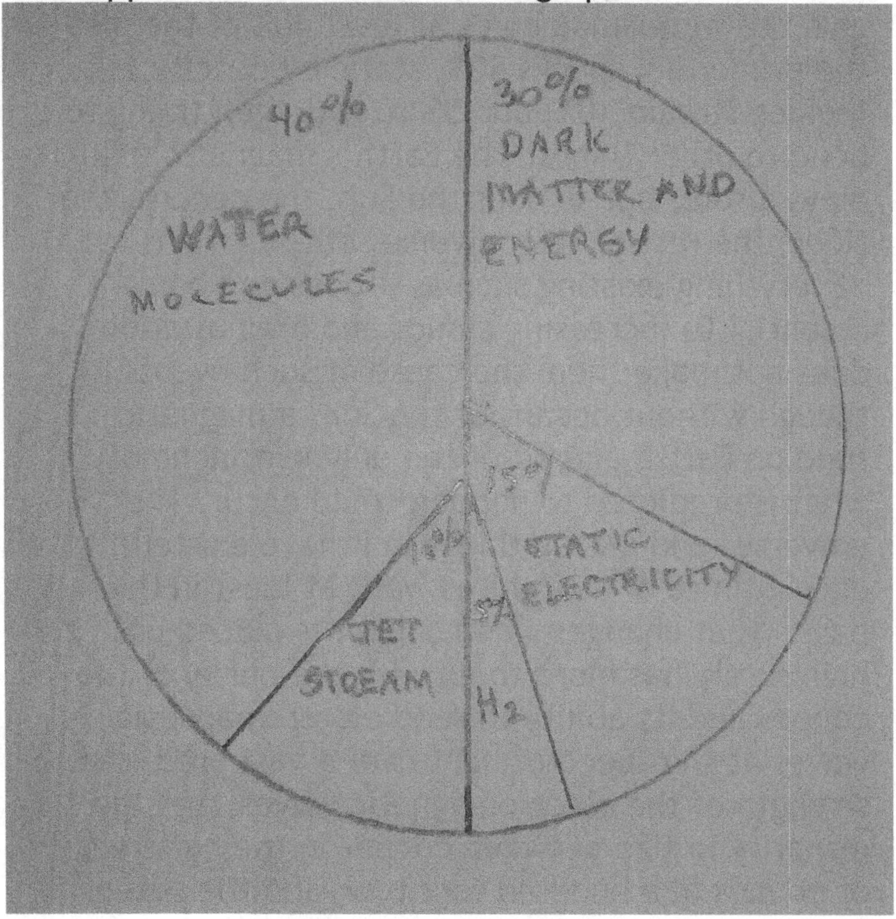

How the pie divides up

Chapter 3: More Cosmology

The simplest explanation must be the truth

JB

The known universe is speeding up its expansion. Common sense tells me that this is happening because there is more matter beyond the known universe exerting a gravitational pull on all that is the known universe. This speeding up of the known universe has gotten a lot of speculation in the astrophysical, astronomical, and cosmological communities.

Astronomers maintain that at one time the known universe had been slowing down as galaxies moved farther away from each other. A huge explosion then high speed ejecta slowing down turned around into accelerating expansion some billions of years ago. Almost all cosmology books written give theories as to why this is happening, none but this one, at least that I have read, supposing simple gravity to be the culprit.

The larger the known universe expands, the weaker becomes the forces existing within the known universe that tend to keep it together gravitationally. The idea that the known universe is not the entire universe, and that matter and energy at a distance of 15 billion light years might not be detectable since the light is too faint suggests itself. The gravitational waves reach us. A guess would give us a possible ratio of how much dark energy and dark mass are local, and how much is matter and energy more distant if one took the totals we have currently. 74% is dark energy, which is the force trying to pull the known universe apart,

22% is dark matter, holding our known universe together, and 4% is currently detected matter and energy, and since matter and energy are both contained within matter initially, and we have 22% dark matter holding us together we probably have here a proportionate share of somewhere around 22% dark energy trying to tear us apart in the local arena, and the other 52% dark energy would consist of the pull of more distant objects upon our ever expanding Big Bang. These more distant things would be objects with matter and energy combined, just like in the known universe. That still leaves us with an 11 to 1 ratio between local dark matter and dark energy, and the known elements.

Astronomer Vera Rubin spent a great deal of time with telescopes measuring the speeds of orbiting stars. She published a paper describing her detailed observations of motions of stars in the Andromeda Galaxy and her conclusion was that "for the stars to be moving with the velocities they had, there would have to be as much as 10 times more mass in the galaxy than was visible."[6] The difference between 10 to 1 and 11 to 1 is only around 1.5%, surprisingly small. Her exact words were 10 times more mass, not mass and energy, but one could take the wider view and assume she meant things, a combination of matter and energy, since that is what exists. Or an amount of dark energy exists to equal the mass.

Other than those figures, there is the chance that our known universe is still in an energetic state; possibly more dark energy is present here, and less is due to distant massive objects. Lots of energy is being released in the stellar activity of 100 billion galaxies. Add to that energy released in supernovae and the argument could be put forth that the gravitational pull of more distant objects accounts for less than 52% of the total dark energy we have yet to find.

Stellar activity and supernovae are not dark energy at all, they are quite known to us, but one could impute more energy to dark matter and dark energy if one were to suppose them to be, or establish that they are, hydrogen precursors. Once they become hydrogen or neutrons, they are then capable of participating in nuclear fusion. Some force is causing the galaxies in the known universe to fly away from each other at increasing speeds, and to clump together in enormous clusters and leave huge empty places in the known universe.

"Mommy, common sense doesn't say anything to me!"

The observations of Vera Rubin point to around a 10 to 1 ratio of primordial specks to known matter and energy, with allowances for her wording, and the proportionality guess gave us 11 to 1, so maybe the figure for dark energy in the known universe could really be 2 or 3 percent higher. The Big Bang occurred, and first began to slow down, then turned into accelerating expansion some billions of years later. Increasing in size, decreasing in density, and as all this happened, the known universe expanded closer to gravitational waves from other massive objects more distant.

The last few years have seen two discoveries that are still being investigated. In 2006, NASA scientists launched a balloon with some sensitive detecting equipment to more closely examine faint radio signals from the most distant stars. What happened was an extremely powerful radio signal from far off totally drowned out any possible signal from the faint stars they were trying to analyze. This radio source was 6 times more powerful than all the radio galaxies in the entire known universe.

What this radio source is can't be on a long list. No doubt it will eventually be concluded to be a big bang in its own right, the light having come and gone, or too faint to see, but the radio waves very strong. I found this article on the internet with the headline “NASA Mystery Boom; Or Something in Space Is Screaming”. I hope that soon, more will be available about this singular discovery. My guess is it hasn't stopped broadcasting powerful radio waves.

Let’s assume that two huge black holes collided at high speed somewhere near the fringes of the known universe, and we are now detecting intense radio waves there from. One would find it likely, even inevitable, that some of the hydrogen pairs in the known universe, those nearest this recent collision between two black holes would come in contact with the cooled plasma from that event before long, and begin to reproduce. Such would have been the case when our known universe began to develop;

some neighboring system of galaxies in existence would have parts that would come in contact with the growing big bang, hydrogen included.

A big bang like the one that created the known universe whose radio waves are now detected but is from so far away that astronomers aren't even sure where it is coming from had to have actually taken place billions of years ago, many light years away. We are now detecting the expanding signals from that event. All the matter and energy appears to be tightly compacted, since the radio waves are so intense, so what we are receiving now would be from two black holes that collided at high speed billions of years ago, and the light therefrom would have seemed like a faint star. The radio waves now indicate a very young big bang, since if the event were older the radio waves would be more diffuse.

At some distant time the known universe was lit up from afar, far greater than a supernova. To suppose that no light shines when two black holes collide at high speed doesn't fit the definition of explosion. I think any significant explosion would release light, and light would be the fastest moving energy escaping the explosion.

Light waves and radio waves both travel at the speed of light, but radio waves would be more continuous, lasting long after light waves from an explosion have come and gone. Distance could have shrunk the size of the explosion to a pinprick of light, not unlike faint stars, from astronomers perspective on Earth. A far away event happens, and isn't known until it reaches Earth, years later. The implications of this discovery could include the possibility that dark matter and dark energy in the known universe are on the increase, even though hydrogen, or neutrons are also on the increase, so actually measuring these quantities precisely now, and a thousand years in the future could show us very little, since quantities of dark, and known matter and energy would both have increased. Many astronomical improvements would have transpired as well. The new distant objects added changes the entire landscape of the known universe. The better detail obtained in 1000 years would change details like total mass and energy, how much is dark, etc.

An article in 2008 by an astronomy team led by Andrew Kashlinsky described what came to be referred to as "Deep Drift". The Centaurus and Saggitarius constellation may overlap in the southern hemisphere, where there is a place the known universe is being pulled toward, galaxies the nearest traveling toward it at extremely high speeds, as much as three million miles per hour, those furthest away much slower.

The entire known universe may be in the grips of a monster black hole. I found this article on the internet as well. If the reader were to search for "Andrew Kashlinsky Article", I'm sure they would find the one about "Deep Drift". Neither article was long or greatly detailed, at least the news stories. Something being discovered from likely outside the boundaries of the known universe, two possibilities, impacts cosmological theory.

Almost all theories in cosmology start with the idea that the known universe is all the universe, that space/time is a fabric of some kind, and that there is something called vacuum energy out of which particles pop out. It could be that a much simpler explanation might be the truth.

Massive objects could still bend light waves even if space/time is not a fabric and space exists independently of time. Photons have been found to have no mass but are definitely something, which came from things with mass, a kind of energy, so space doesn't need to be a fabric. Light waves are pulled by gravity. How a force can reach through empty space is beyond me, yet common sense says that is what is happening. Space doesn't change, a force moves across space.

It makes the most sense that it would be a wave traveling at the speed of light, which is the current view. The failure of light to escape a black hole is surely due to the intense gravitational force of the black hole, not some change in the fabric of space.

A black hole will have a specific diameter; ten feet away from the outer surface of the black hole the gravitational waves would be extremely intense passing through empty space. Black holes are thus not holes, they are entities of specific diameter that no light escapes. No matter how tightly squeezed, a black hole occupies space. Wormhole fantasy can be excluded. That light does not emerge from a black hole shows us light waves are subject to gravity.

The more distant an object in the known universe is from us, the faster it is receding from us since the more distant it is, the closer it is to undetected massive objects, hence the more distant objects are influenced by the gravity of these other massive objects hitherto undetected. For the entire universe to be contained within the Big Bang and now, after almost 14 billion years, the entire collection of 100 billion galaxies is not slowing down as it flies farther and farther away from where everything in the known universe was when the Big Bang occurred makes no sense at all in the context of the natural laws as we know them, with the known universe all that exists.

Gravity would have begun to slow the expansion in time, so now theorists are inventing repulsive gravity to explain the excess of dark energy. More likely normal gravity, just elsewhere. We have neighbors on the fringes of the known universe, and possibly more further away. The mass they contain could round things out. Hence the Big Bang most likely didn't happen as theories now state. In fact, exactly what we are observing would be true; dark energy would be much higher than dark matter if a huge amount of matter were too far away to detect, yet were exerting a gravitational pull.

If we throw away those assumptions, the known universe being the entire universe, space/time being a fabric of some kind, and particles popping out of vacuum energy, and in the words of Henry David Thoreau, simplify, simplify, we perhaps answer these questions, at least as well as we can.

From what I can gather there is a problem in physics concerning uniting the force of gravity with existing theories, and maybe new insights into the probable location of the excess 52% dark energy, and where the missing particle can be found to concentrate which makes up somewhere from 90 to 92% of all the matter and energy in our known universe, and is the primordial speck, can help scientists solve that puzzle.

At present, more and more exotic theories are emerging to try to bring successful answers to questions such as what happened in the first few seconds of the Big Bang, why the known universe is speeding up in its expansion, and what and where dark matter and dark energy are. The complexity and unusualness of these theories is a sure sign that some simplification is overdue. There are several books I read that had ideas in cosmology that were so weird they weren't worth mentioning.

The notion of space/time as some kind of a coexistent fabric came about originally as part of Einstein's Theory of Relativity. That theory and its predictions still hold true even if space and time turn out to be something other than the coexistent fabric it has been supposed to be.

flip my egg, and it is soon done

From the beginning of language, events and things were seen in the real world to take place and have what would seem to be duration, continuance. We now have many words to indicate amounts of time. Something changes from when an egg is raw to when it is cooked, beside fire being applied to it.

The fire is applied so long or the egg is burnt. Describing the passage of time is difficult without referring to it, as in the "so long" referring to how much time passes. These same events, to be perceived, had dimension also, in effect they were large enough to be visible to human eyes. Besides that, there was certainly a lot of space around. Even if the ancients didn't have the astronomical knowledge we do now, space was all around, and distances were calculated, maps made to scale.

Philosophers mused over space and time quite a bit way back when, some decided time and space were immutable absolutes, eternal, unchanging, or something like that. Others claimed they didn't exist. The problem of space and time is that they are not tangible things, made of known elements. Space not having any features other than being a frictionless medium through which any and all matter and energy can travel, it isn't a something.

There is an up, down, left and right direction anywhere we have found. The dimensions of space are emptiness. One would have to build a wall to impede movement. The void is increate, and anywhere that matter and energy may travel, they find nothing but emptiness. The coordinates are there, and it is extremely doubtful that space itself consists of anything more than that. There is an x and y axis anywhere one might imagine, irrespective of matter and energy, which may or may not be present at whatever coordinates. There are no space coordinates anywhere imaginable that aren't there, no place with no space.

Time has a unique kind of existence. The universe has things in it, they are traveling through space, and one moment continually gives on to the next. It seems there would be no other way for the things in the universe to travel, but for movement to arrive at a new destination after lapse of time. Time can't not exist, but it is what must be to permit the movement of things, just as space is.

We see that as a thing moves, it goes from one place to another. Space and Time couldn't not be there for that to happen, therefore Time exists as a consequence of there being moving things, and Space couldn't not be there were something to move into whatever spatial coordinates. If nothing moved anywhere, no time would elapse.

Something moves. It winds up in another location. There are measurable increments of time involved in its moving, but these increments only exist in the minds of those that have conceived of them. Where things moved had nothing else in it but the matter and energy that moved, through an increate void. Time wasn't there, other than as a conceptual measurement that was possible for intelligent observers to make. Things have been in motion through space for all eternity, observed or not.

Time, then, isn't a something of any kind. That humans can measure how long it takes the Earth to orbit the Sun doesn't change the fact that the only things existing are matter and energy moving through the increate void.

A space ship leaving Earth and traveling near the speed of light for 100 years upon then returning to Earth will find family and friends long dead, though only about five years or so would have elapsed to the inhabitants of the spacecraft. This tells us there is theoretically a variable factor in time, though not a very practical one for human intents and purposes. Time appears to be ever moving forward, slower in the space craft than on Earth.

Space is where all this takes place, the spaceship would have traveled an incredible distance, but space could still be an immutable absolute, in short, the edges of the universe do not exist, for there is no way for space to not exist. Speed of travel seems to slow down time, and it takes extreme speeds to do that to any extent. The event surely happened in space, but speed of travel, not variability of space, is what caused it.

Speculating upon why that effect should occur if the void is increate gives the inevitable conclusion that speeds approaching the speed of light are so fast that the universe is incapable of creating increments of time small enough to account for every inch of movement.

If a living thing could travel that fast, the being may be outrunning time by a considerable extent, each second traveling nearly 186,000 miles. Time can't keep up. Even the notion that time slows down at speeds approaching the speed of light could be based on faulty assumptions, since it is only theoretically possible, and impossible to prove.

A solar eclipse occurred in 1919 where Einstein predicted the light from stars that are behind the Sun from our vantage point would bend as they passed by near the Sun, and astronomers confirmed that is what happened. This was the main proof of the space/time continuum idea.

I think it more likely space stays the same and the photons change course. The force of gravity is still not understood, and assigning change to what is eternal and unchanging sends one in the wrong direction. If light waves cannot escape a black hole, they would also be pulled toward stars by gravity.

Whatever force field or wave gravity is, perhaps also lays beyond our instruments to comprehend other than as some kind of quantum mechanical probability. What happens to the photon, with no mass, considered to exhibit properties of both a particle and a wave, could be simply owing to its existing, being energy, even without mass. Photons are being pulled by gravity, preserving the nobility of space. No evidence proves conclusively that space need change in any way.

A lot of physics math calculations scientists do involve space, x and y axis type equations, and it is very convenient and expedient for equations that involve space and time to factor the two in together. I'm really not sure if that isn't what Einstein meant by space/time. It is a construct to facilitate one's better understanding of the processes that works well with equations, but the reality is space is flat and completely empty until something enters it, and being nothing, passively permits passage. The coordinates are all existing.

Black holes are the recyclers of the universe. The second law of thermodynamics states that entropy within a system will always increase. The universe is always bound for more disorder.

The only time or place where entropy doesn't increase, one could argue, is within a black hole. Within these strange entities gravitational forces prevent anything from escaping, and the pressure is so great that molecular bonds are broken. They are a system unto themselves, and exert a strong gravitational force on other things in the universe.

Everything that comes within range of a black hole will be absorbed by it, and be converted into a part of the homogeneous whole. A twenty billion year old light wave, incredibly faint, spread very thinly, when absorbed by a black hole, changes to part of the plasma within the black hole. Entropy decreases, as a total quantity throughout the entire universe, when that occurs. A forty billion year old chunk of matter, adrift in space at near absolute zero, when absorbed by a black hole, becomes part of the plasma within the black hole. Entropy again decreases. Any and every time some matter and energy is absorbed by a black hole, a very compacted, unchanging entity replaces all the myriad things that the matter and energy just were, occupying considerably more space.

Part of the second law of thermodynamics is the flow of heat toward a colder region from a hotter one. Dissipation of heat is always occurring in the known universe that we occupy. Something warmer than its surroundings dissipates heat, something cooler than the surrounding area does not.

Not true of black holes, since gravity is so strong nothing escapes. Ten feet from a black hole, I'm assuming it is cold. Not a place one could visit to see if heat is dissipating from the black hole.

Once a black hole becomes large enough and collides with another at high speed, the objects being the only significant objects of mass over a very large area, all the plasma is released in an explosion such as the Big Bang, and galaxies form with energy in abundance, planets with liquid water, life, etc. Repeatedly cycles of systems of galaxies form, in time burn themselves out, are absorbed by black holes, and in many other places two black holes collide, and the cycle repeats.

In the whole universe multiple such events would come and go over eons. Any kind of unique events could also happen, like two black holes colliding, with a third black hole on a collision course with the other two that arrives a thousand years late, and ends up tripling in size in a short time.

As theorized, hydrogen has supplanted any other possible reproducing entity when plasma from a Big Bang has cooled sufficiently; some hydrogen isotopes wander in from afar, and these serve as templates, and eventually hydrogen is the most abundant element in that part of the universe, upon which heavier elements are based.

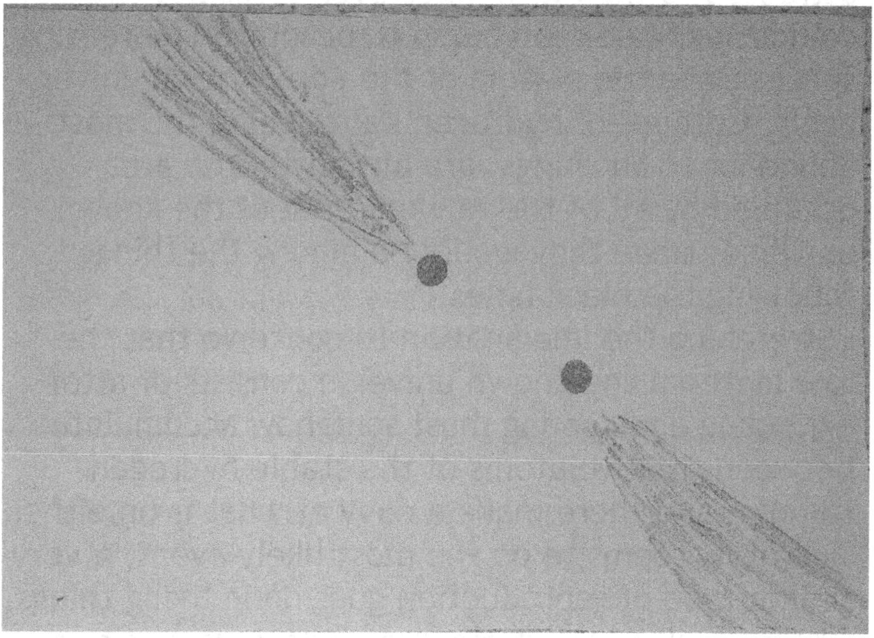

Two black holes one second before collision, H2 in pursuit

How things happened in the early universe with regard to whether the first hydrogen atoms developed spontaneously or drifted in from afar might be explained by the behavior of the two black holes before colliding. Gravity had to be pulling the black holes toward each other for some time, so the two objects accelerated as they approached each other. Objects within range of the gravitational fields of the two black holes would still be heading towards the black holes from all sides.

The black holes are now accelerating, so some of the things that came within range of either would fall behind it, so each would have a tail similar to a comet's tail as it accelerates around the sun, but much larger. This tail of things following the two black holes would continue to be gravitationally attracted to the black holes even after the two collide, explode, and begin to occupy an increasing space. Once the plasma of the early known universe cools, isotopes of hydrogen pairs, being the most abundant of all things, are already in the area occupied by all of the raw material of the known universe, since they would be among the things following the black holes.

Stretching the imagination to conceive that the raw material the known universe consists of after exploding and cooling must somehow accumulate between the two atoms of the stable hydrogen isotope, and there make a copy of what is on either side of it, seems to be the most likely event; a very similar type of reproduction goes on in living things, where a cellular part emerges from between two identical copies. The tiniest things existing flow into the tiny space between the two atoms of the stable hydrogen isotope, and because of the proximity on either side of identical things emitting intense beams of energy, a third hydrogen atom coalesces.

There is information transfer, the primordial specks assimilate the information and gain the identity of a single hydrogen atom, or a neutron. The isotope briefly becomes a triplet of simple hydrogen, and then the hydrogen atom is cut loose, to pair up with a like atom. If a neutron is the embryo, some other stages occur to make hydrogen atoms. That puts the hydrogen atom itself into a class of its own, since it reproduces as pairs. The simplest atom alone is the one capable of it, as stable pairs. Hydrogen is the starting point for all the other elements also, so it is a really busy little thing. One could liken them to an ant colony of the most primitive type.

The cycle from black holes to systems of galaxies and back isn't perfectly repeating, all the matter from the universe will be spread out into more systems of galaxies and black holes than we will ever be able to see, with no walls in between.

Therefore, the matter from one system of galaxies, as it burns out and is slowly absorbed by black holes, could wind up in a dozen or more different new systems of galaxies eventually depending on where gravity takes the various parts of the system of galaxies burning out.

The entire universe is too large for each Big Bang to be an exact replica of the previous, since there would be many such events unfolding at all times. Earth is existing for the first time, not the billionth time. Many planets similar to Earth may have come and gone, but similarities, and not exact repetition, are more likely. Maybe eternity would see a repeat.

In such a large system as 100 billion galaxies, size would certainly vary between black holes that collide, and black holes near to the system of galaxies could vary in distance and direction to the system of galaxies, changing the momentum of things uniquely in each instance. It is highly unlikely that two cruising black holes in the depths of space would ever collide again with the exact amount of matter and energy to the last gram.

Nothing disobeys the 2nd law of thermodynamics, according to current views in physics, yet black holes seem to, and the fact anything absorbed by a black hole is reduced to a plasma under intense pressure is the process that keeps the universe able to create new systems of galaxies through black holes colliding at high speed. Black holes are at the centers of nearly all galaxies and are growing. What that implies is that these black holes aren't just going to fizzle one moment and cease to exist; growth will continue until all the matter and energy that continually goes in them comes out in an explosion. That type of event happening many times before in the universe seems likely.

The current Standard Model in physics that is widely accepted is that from 3 to 20 minutes into the Big Bang, temperatures and pressures fell far enough to create first hydrogen, then deuterium, deuterium combine through fusion into $helium_4$, and some $Helium_4$ combine to make a very small amount of $lithium_7$. After 20 minutes, all the baryons in the universe were created. What remains is mostly hydrogen, from 10 to 20% helium, and a small amount of lithium. All the other elements arise through processes in stars.

It is here in the Standard Model that we find a different distribution of elements than the 93% hydrogen ordinarily seen. Only 86% is hydrogen, and most of the rest is helium. I still wonder which figure is correct, and why there are two figures for how much hydrogen in existence. When the twenty minute period ended there was 86% hydrogen, and now 93% hydrogen would seem to indicate more hydrogen came along later. That would negate the theory that all heavy particles were created in the first twenty minutes after the Big Bang.

The first and foremost problem with that theory is whatever the scientists suppose caused the Big Bang in the first place; some assume that some ripple in the quantum field just caused expansion, or inflation. Black holes will continue to grow in the known universe and are certainly, through high speed collision after eons of growth, the cause of the Big Bang, from any number of groups of galaxies that burned out long before the Big Bang.

A supernova in the middle ages raged for several years during which time it was possible to read by the light from there on cloudless nights. No light bulbs then. One star exploding for several years means two black holes colliding at high speed may have an explosion that lasts as long as a decade.

Hard to figure where to put that 3 to 20 minutes, where all the baryons were supposedly created by the Higgs boson. After the explosion dies out, things are still hot, heat not escaping from the black holes for billions of years, so even then, nothing stable would develop until everything cooled.

Explosions, however big or small, involve things contained in a small space suddenly occupying a growing space, individual parts becoming further apart. Things are not coming together under such conditions, they are being torn asunder. Shock waves from such a tremendous explosion would ripple along, turning the plasma into ever smaller bits. Magnetic monopoles are all remaining, once the explosion dies out. From the death of the explosion a smaller black hole may remain. After temperatures fall the magnetic monopoles join in myriad forms, none remaining stable for more than a few millionths of a second. Some hydrogen could, conceivably, begin to exist spontaneously in the early stages when the plasma is very dense.

Two black holes colliding could release more heat than Standard Model Big Bang temperatures by far. A recent science channel presentation on television gave the temperature of a supernova at about 100 billion degrees. A huge black hole, dissipating no heat for 850 billion years, growing all the while, collides with an even bigger black hole that has been absorbing things from the universe for almost 2 trillion years, also dissipating no heat all the while. The temperature of the explosion, trillions of degrees. Two black holes colliding is hotter by far than current estimates of the Big Bang, based on whatever foolishness.

The Standard Model and its idea all baryons in existence are created in 20 minutes spontaneously, also includes the spontaneous development of anti-matter through the same process. No anti-matter galaxies are now visible from Earth. That does call into question whether ordinary hydrogen developed spontaneously, since there should be an equal amount of anti-hydrogen, anti-helium, and if they are not there, the idea is wrong.

Scientists could argue regular matter won the battle between the two, and all anti-matter was destroyed by contact in the early years of the known universe, but it makes no sense. The battle that may have raged between hydrogen and other possible entities that might have done the same thing as hydrogen, reproduce themselves in the primordial soup of a recent big bang, is over, and we don’t know what the other contestants were, or if such a battle ever developed, and how long ago. It is unlikely that 96% of the universe is debris, and the space between hydrogen atoms yielding a neutron is so small an event it has not been noticed.

Entropy increases throughout the time energy and matter are thrown out of a black hole, until such time as that matter and energy returns to a black hole. Entropy then decreases. A very hot, pressurized, uniform plasma inside a small area is a more orderly arrangement than huge numbers of massive objects of varying sizes cast out over billions of light years and releasing energy, planets with living things, etc. Things grow more and more complex as more interactions between elements occurs; hardly the case when those same things are squeezed into a plasma for a trillion years.

Things stay the same within a black hole, the only change would be a growth in size, or a collision with another black hole. The centers of most if not all galaxies is thought to be a black hole. Some collisions must occur in the universe between black holes that aren't super massive enough to create billions of galaxies, since in our known universe, there are nearly 100 billion black holes, one at the center of every galaxy.

The likelihood is that in one system of galaxies such as our own, galaxies orbit each other in clusters and when two galaxies merge, the black holes at the centers of the galaxies won't head straight toward each other and would merge into a larger black hole at the center of a bigger galaxy. The Milky Way and the Andromeda Galaxy are going to combine, or collide, over millions of years. Black holes in our known universe after more billions of years will combine with more black holes and become super massive black holes once stars burn out and finally there would only be a few left.

There is one other explanation that fits observed large structures in the universe to some extent. Smaller black hole collisions, occurring at slower speeds than those involving very large black holes, might not be able to completely overcome the intense gravitational field of the two black holes recently united. The now single black hole doesn't explode, but begins to vent plasma from opposite ends, similarly to the cosmic beams of stars after a supernova, but on a much more gigantic scale.

Clusters of galaxies presently identified exhibit the shape of filaments, long clusters of galaxies only a few dozen million light years in diameter, but over a billion light years in length. There are also dark matter and energy plumes crossing the cosmos, and where two of these plumes intersect there is always a cluster of galaxies found there.

Therefore, three types of events involving black holes appear to be happening in the universe. One would be the granddaddy of all explosions, like the Big Bang, where two black holes collide at speeds high enough to bring about an intense explosion. The second would involve black holes on a smaller scale, at slower speeds, colliding, and combining, but with enough of an impact to cause the now single black hole to vent plasma from opposite ends, lasting from a month to as long as a decade. Thirdly, some black holes combine peacefully, not exploding, and venting plasma only for a short while or not at all, and with the large number of them known, bound to happen sometimes. There are around 40 super clusters of galaxies identified, mostly within two billion light years. Millions more super clusters of galaxies exist certainly, further distant. Where matter and energy goes is from whence it will eventually reemerge. It seems black holes are the conduits for matter and energy, in by gravity and out by the events just described. There are also large voids where only a galaxy or two can be found, and some of the nearer large voids in the cosmos have been identified.

Distance is the reason only 40 super clusters and about a dozen or so voids have been found. Consider trying to establish the boundary of a structure or void at distances beyond two billion light years; resolution is poor and the difficulty of calculating distances so immense that it seems almost impossible. After many years of data from orbiting satellites a clearer picture might emerge.

The Big Bang could have been more than one cataclysmic event over the last 14 billion years or so. If a big bang occurs between two black holes every two billion years or so, a half dozen or so may have happened in our quadrant, and if that all took place within a larger universe, the pull of the rest of the universe would have all observable matter heading away from us at increasing speeds, just as we see now. All the things of the universe flying through space always results in black holes eventually colliding and releasing new energy.

There would really be no differences between one big bang around 14 billion years ago and half a dozen of them spread out over the same number of years. The first one occurs, and stars are hardly formed before there is a second, and by the time of the third collision between black holes, the known universe increases its production of hydrogen with the additional material and an additional trickle of hydrogen or neutrons into the known universe results. The microwave background radiation might tell us more about that, but I don't know for sure. If there were a big bang less than 3 billion years ago, surely the background radiation from the event would have waves that were less elongated than background radiation from much longer ago. But if all background radiation is the same, that would rule out multiple big bangs unless we are only detecting background radiation from the most recent big bang, and all the previous ones are now too faint to detect at all.

The known universe is so huge I'm guessing there could have been more than one colossal explosion over the billions of years that our known universe has been around, in its current state. Maybe the most recent was 5 billion years ago, and that is all we detect, and it was the fifth such event in the known universe. Black holes seem to be able to grow indefinitely, and it is possible two large black holes were responsible for all in the known universe.

However it all happened, with dark matter and dark energy occupying such a high percentage of all that exists in the known universe one could argue that this suggests that perhaps not all matter within the known universe was contained within one big bang, since if it were, more atoms of hydrogen, or neutrons, would have surely evolved by now, that event happening almost 14 billion years ago.

The lack of developed hydrogen suggests some of the known universe might have come along more recently, with less time for hydrogen or neutrons to develop, and has conjoined with what was here before. The galaxies we can see are from the first few events, and most of the dark matter and dark energy that is now intertwined with the galaxies came along more recently on the cosmic scale.

The scientific view is that the known universe is all the same age. 13.6 or so billion years ago was when it all started. However, conceding that the known universe does appear to be that age, if one Big Bang occurred then, and subsequent explosions later conjoined with the first, the later black hole events would begin to produce hydrogen just like the first event, and be identical to the hydrogen atoms of the first. A trickle of more hydrogen or neutrons occurring wouldn't change the age of the known universe, if it can really be accurately pinned down in the first place.

The standard model view posits the observable universe to be about 93 billion light years in diameter. A distance of 46.5 billion light years in every direction, quite a bit bigger than a Big Bang occurring 13.6 billion years ago could have traveled at the speed of light, based upon the assumption that space/time underwent cosmic inflation and is still expanding, and anything beyond 46.5 billion light years will never come in contact with us.

In other words, if we could see that far, we might see things a distance of 46.5 billion light years, but we would not see anything further since the light from anything further away than 46.5 billion light years would not reach us. Things further than 46.5 billion light years are undergoing spatial expansion to the extent it is receding so fast that nothing from there reaches us. The Hubble Telescope was credited in January of 2011 with finding the most distant galaxy ever, 13.2 billion light years away.

If one takes the view that space is but empty dimension, gravity could extend indefinitely. Light would be too faint to detect moving through space for more than 15 billion years. Gravity from some extremely massive thing 60 billion light years away could alter the course of the known universe, albeit to a lesser extent than something of the same size 30 billion light years distant. The things in our known universe could eventually meet something from that far away, with enough time.

The universe doesn't look to be lacking when it comes to time, there is no end in sight. The space time concept puts us in a bubble, separate from other bubbles of matter and energy elsewhere, an odd situation when all matter and energy is moving, with inertia, and gravity is a wave extending at the speed of light. The supposed bubbles, collections of matter and energy, intertwine and crisscross.

Galaxies that are observable now are each being slowly absorbed by the black hole at the center of each. Since super clusters of galaxies orbit around each other, in time the black holes will combine. In the end, however many remaining black holes head off in opposite directions, being already far apart in the expanding known universe, towards other black holes from other systems of galaxies.

After however many billions of years, there are a few thousand black holes remaining to our known universe, and they all drift off toward other objects of mass elsewhere in the entire universe, and keep growing until they are so large that a significant area of space lies between them and a like object toward which the black hole is pulled, resulting in considerable speeds and a huge impact.

100 billion black holes currently in the known universe, all of which will combine with other black holes until such time as the black holes are so large and far apart that any further meeting results in huge speeds and a terrific explosion. Some vent

plasma on combining, but growth of a decreasing number of black holes over eons would result. The matter and energy of the universe will never reveal its full extent to us, and could continue into the depths of space endlessly. More black holes, more galaxies where black holes collided.

Contrary to popular belief then, perpetual motion is possible, all one needs are the forces of nature as we know them. The fact that the entire universe is, and is here now, confirms this. The simplest explanation for how it is the wilderness we call the universe exists is that it always has. No special contrivances are needed for perpetual motion to have always existed.

If it is a true depiction of reality, that the universe is a system in perpetual motion, by dint of being incredibly large, then it existing now means it had to have existed at any past time. Removing something that large would take a lot of doing; there has ever been any agency capable of it. Just as there is no end to the future, there is also no end to the past. The various things that exist have never not existed.

The law of conservation of energy, that energy is conserved within a system, holds at all times in the entire universe, no doubt. The universe probably hasn't changed an ounce in total weight ever. Time travel will prove an impossibility. The fantasy of time travel, when one just takes into account the speed at which the solar system travels with the Milky Way, is a bit farfetched.

Just ten minutes ago, Earth was over 220,000 miles from where it is now. Ten minutes hence, the Earth will be 220,000 plus miles distant; the inexorable march of the universe cannot be stopped, and going backward or forward in time is absurd. There is no past to go back to, matter and energy from there has gone onward to the present, the only time frame where matter and energy can be found. Travel back to the place Earth was 10 minutes ago, and the Earth is not there any longer. The only past that exists, exists in the minds of intelligent beings aware of time, and whatever records and memories that have been kept.

Race ahead to where we will be 10 minutes in the future, and Earth and all its creatures won't be there until they get there. The universe will march on in the inexorable present as it always has, huge, uncaring, an utter wilderness. That makes the cells of our bodies the oldest things in existence, quite eternal, as all the matter and energy in the universe is also. The things we are made of have traversed to and from black holes countless times.

One could speculate that after eons of time the things that make up the universe might evolve through experience to some extent, and that the big bang that we are a part of now is very different than a big bang that occurred billions and billions of cycles of black holes and systems of galaxies ago. That question won't be answered without going to the distant past, something humans will never do.

Explosions of the magnitude of big bangs reduce things in the universe to such small things there is no chance of retaining any information from the past, so it could be that the current state of the known universe is not at all unlike a system of galaxies that developed a very, very long time ago.

Once the Solar System is swallowed by a black hole, and eventually reemerges in a collision with another black hole, the eventual unities of structure like living things would seldom have more than a pound or two of matter and energy from any one of billions of previously existing galaxies, and each of the little bits and pieces could have been parts of any number of stars or planets or other inanimate things, with much less than one percent likely having been part of a living thing. All the plasma within a black hole is the same thing. Once something entered it, it is not star 29 in the galaxy such and such, it is plasma, the same as the rest of the black hole.

The idea of inspiration coming from our eternal being, various parts of which may have once been part of some previously existing intelligent being, is pretty unlikely, but can't be entirely ruled out. Residual traces of things appear everywhere, perhaps with regard to previous experiences, and how new thoughts emerge.

I doubt the universe would be able to do much else besides create huge systems of galaxies from black holes colliding. Some cosmology books get real far out when it comes to explaining what is happening at vast distances. Vast distances from us the laws of nature will operate just as here. Any place else in the whole universe where black holes have collided various spheres develop, originally containing little but hydrogen and neutrons, these spheres continue to grow, and nuclear fusion, heavier elements, planets, and life all begin. When two black holes collide and the 2nd law of thermodynamics begins to operate, it will always result in a scenario similar to what we have in the known universe. Black holes that recently united, venting plasma, are freeing that plasma from the intense gravitational collapse of the now united black holes. The 2nd law of thermodynamics would also begin to operate with respect to the vented plasma. It is no longer under intense gravitational collapse, and will come in contact with hydrogen in time.

Extrapolating from what we can observe to be occurring to the conclusion that such events are ordinary seems reasonable. We will never know for certain what happens in other areas of the universe beyond the known universe, or for that matter most of the known universe. That does not mean we cannot develop a keen sense of how the universe must in all probability exist in places we will never see, except telescopically in some instances.

We can make assumptions about things whose exact specific details we will never know by knowing the laws of physics, the nature of the Void, expanding the size of the universe, and the time frame through which it operates, eternity.

That simplifies the universe considerably, in light of all the confusion over its origin, always when did the Big Bang occur, never does the possibility arise that the Big Bang was not the first or only such type event in the entire universe. The second law of thermodynamics always comes to operate when two black holes collide and explode.

After stars develop for billions of years, and life develops on many planets, the system of galaxies runs out of fuel, and burns out. Black holes absorb the waste material, slowly combine, and eventually grow so large that a collision between two of them would start such a process over again.

The complexity of things in the universe comes from the very small size individual components can be. The human brain has 10 billion neurons, each one a cell with millions of atoms of hydrogen, carbon, nitrogen, oxygen and other elements. The complexity of the universe can only reach its highest plateau through living things. We have no idea what level of complexity other living beings may have reached throughout the endless past. It could even be possible that black holes and systems of galaxies have come about with different things within them other than hydrogen, and hydrogen is the creation of some advanced race that seeded the known universe with a synthetic creation of its own when the Big Bang occurred, or countless eons ago it was mixed in a lab, escaped and survives, and is completely ubiquitous in the entire universe now.

All humanity can do with regard to the past is speculate; that hydrogen is here is known, but how and when it developed into what appears to be the only thing capable of reproducing itself among fragments from a big bang is not something we can establish, other than to suppose that at one time there was no hydrogen, and some later time it

Except for the little stuff

developed. One can't be sure even of that, if all eternity has existed with hydrogen present.

Whether or not life can evolve to the level of advancement where the extremely advanced living things could actually change the outcome of what begins to exist when black holes collide is never going to be established for certain, but it seems to be theoretically possible. That also seems to be the extent of what the universe is capable of.

Nothing other than intelligent beings that evolved over long periods of time could possibly change the development of things once two black holes explode, and then only by a good stretch of the imagination. The process of matter and energy being stored in black holes for really long periods of time and eventually colliding with another black hole and releasing all that matter and energy seems such an inexorable series of events involving such extremely huge systems of things that it seems that no intelligent being would ever be able to do anything other than to avoid a black hole with spacecraft.

The current Big Bang theory, that everything, including space and time, came from a singularity, gives us a catalyst for the explosion known as the Big Bang. Space, time, all matter and energy can't compress indefinitely. Something gives. If space couldn't have changed, and not all existing was condensed into the supposed singularity since there are other objects of mass and energy beyond the known universe, which couldn't be there without space and time, a necessary corollary of things existing, then the theory doesn't explain the Big Bang, and there is no catalyst for the explosion. The collision of two enormous black holes at high speed gives us the missing catalyst. It also gives us continuity. To suppose that prior to the big bang there was nothing, isn't taking known facts to reasonable or inevitable conclusions.

We have no idea how large the universe in its entirety is, and never will establish any edge to all existing with any certainty. An entire universe 1000 times bigger than the known universe would have a collision between black holes resulting in an explosion like the Big Bang occurring on average an estimated once every 250,000,000 years, while an entire universe extending much further could have a Big Bang type event every 100,000 years on average. The larger the entire universe, the more often such events would happen, throughout the entire arena of things existing.

Now that we have the evidence from the NASA discovery in 2006 of powerful radio waves, chances are good that this could prove to be a big bang in its own right. Returning to the Grand Unified Theory of a single unified force being split apart and as a consequence enormous numbers of magnetic monopoles being created by the Big Bang, that theory would work if the single unified force existed within black holes before they collide. As we've shown, things within a black hole would be basically the same and mimics exactly what the theory of the Big Bang started as, a very hot plasma. That everything in a black hole is subject to a single unified force before it collides and explodes makes sense, it is all one type of thing.

The magnetic monopoles my theory says should be there are the smallest things that could possibly exist, can't be reduced to anything smaller, what the plasma of the Big Bang consisted of. The single unified force splits into the strong nuclear force, the electromagnetic force, the gravitational force, and the weak interactions. The weak interactions involve radioactive decay, and it took the known universe some billions of years before radioactive elements developed, but one would have to assume that the potential for that force was possible once the Big Bang occurred, and the second law of thermodynamics began to operate. Radioactive isotopes of smaller elements that decayed rapidly have existed earlier in the universe at times, so weak interactions would have been occurring anytime a radioactive isotope developed during supernova.

A neighboring Big Bang would create magnetic monopoles just like any other, and since the radio waves from the NASA Mystery Boom are here, chances are pretty good we are now being flooded by additional magnetic monopoles ready to turn into hydrogen, or neutrons.

The Sun may increase stellar activity as a result and we could be on our way back to a swamp like Earth in just a few thousand years. More hydrogen on Earth means more water, melting ice caps, more swamps and higher temperatures. We have no idea how long this other thing has been there. Could be all possible effects from introduction of more hydrogen precursors to our known universe have already come and things have stabilized. Humans may have just noticed it recently, but it is surely billions of years old. The discovery in 2006 should in time point to that event being responsible for a lot of our current dark matter and dark energy.

Since detecting the individual particles that make up the dark matter and dark energy is thus far impossible, we would only be able to roughly estimate how many are likely to exist in a given area. The atmosphere of Earth should have a similar percentage of undetectable particles as anywhere else, but then Earth is a small celestial body. It could be fewer dark particles are here on Earth because Earth's gravitational field isn't as strong as the gravitational fields of stars.

There could also be dense clouds of dark matter and energy adrift in the depths of space through which the Earth could occasionally pass, plumes of dark matter and dark energy from a venting black hole, changing amounts in the atmosphere, and possibly causing other significant changes, especially with regards to the climate. Ice ages could come and go depending upon our position with respect to a dark matter and dark energy plume in deep space that Earth exited or entered.

Supposing the Earth to ordinarily only have around 40% as much dark particulates as stellar concentrations, and then the Solar System drifts into a dense cloud of these dark particulates, tripling the quantities present in the atmosphere, rain would get more plentiful, clouds more abundant, and the Earth could careen into an ice age, without the real cause properly understood.

If hydrogen or neutrons are ever conclusively proven to come about as hypothesized here, and a calculated amount of additional hydrogen or neutrons were found in a vacuum chamber that originally had some hydrogen isotopes within to serve as templates, it probably doesn't mean that the amount of hydrogen or neutrons being created on a daily basis will always be the same. One would have to keep a vacuum chamber experiment going on a daily schedule, in case the quantity being created changes dramatically. It would be important to get as much information as possible about the relative abundance of primordial specks in the atmosphere at any one time.

After all, the Earth is flying along through the wilderness, and an untold number of things could await it, including asteroids, meteors, rogue planets, huge plumes of dark matter and dark energy, brown dwarf stars, cosmic beams from supernova, and eventually a black hole.

In a Cosmological sense, the observation that the lighter elements within the core of the Earth are always making their way toward the surface that is a factor in the growth of volcanoes has tremendous implications when one considers whether or not it is likely that there is other life in the universe.

If supernovae create heavier elements, and planets get created at the same time, many such planets would have similar experiences. The huge chunks of molten stellar material that eventually became Earth and Mars came from a Blue Giant or other type star in a supernova. The end result was our Sun, at the center of a solar system with planets, moons, asteroids, and comets emerging.

Mars being smaller than Earth, and farther from the Sun, solidification of the surface would have happened more quickly than Earth, and volcanism would have brought the lighter elements to the surface just like Earth. That means Mars was very Earth like with liquid water on its surface as far back as a few hundred million years before the first micro-organisms appeared on Earth.

Some scenarios describing the early solar system assume the planets just begin to eventually clump together after a supernova, from dust and small fragments. Twenty miles beneath our feet, our planet is hot enough to liquefy metal. It would seem the planets were more likely huge chunks of stellar material thrown out of the supernova amid debris that was continually falling into them in the early going. The outer surface of the planet eventually solidifies, trapping lighter elements within, and they head for the surface.

Comets aren't really necessary for the Earth or Mars to have water. Water would have been among the very first things exiting the interior of the planet, after the crust solidified, and in the early stages of the Earth steam vents would have been common. Less water emerges from volcanoes now because it was lighter than what remains and is now mostly gone. Geysers don't spew out water from inside the Earth, it is surface water reused.

Having all the lighter elements and the propensity of the lighter elements to grow as more complex chains of molecular compounds brings us to right about where Earth was when life appeared. On Mars, some amino acids could have developed just as here, and with some entity able to reproduce itself, it began to do so, or some polymer made the breakthrough of making copies of itself, and eventually whatever this reproducing entity was grows further in complexity until it could be said to be a living organism. I've seen the statement that amino acids are small engines in themselves, and each would have different mechanisms that a living thing with various parts could put to use.

Recently a program aired about the search for the origins of life, the DNA molecule, and the genetic code, and the conclusion reached was that the whole thing could be replicated and would turn out to be pretty simple, but one would need to know what the very first steps were. What thing gained complexity and became a living thing.

Naturally occurring phospholipid molecules have two ends, one hydrophobic, the other hydrophilic. When these molecules are placed in water what happens is that they naturally arrange themselves in a membranous ball, with the water seeking ends of the molecules facing out and the water avoiding ends aligned to the inside of the ball. Cellular life must have taken early advantage of this natural phenomenon since cell membranes are still very similarly designed.

Multi-cellular life might not have been possible without phospholipid molecules. Some polymer succeeds in making copies of itself. One of these is enveloped by phospholipid molecules. The polymer reproduces again, the two entities move away from each other, and the ball of phospholipids splits into two balls, one now enveloping each of the two polymers. Populations of this thing, not quite life yet, begin to develop after time. Some wind up separated from others of its kind by some distance and encounter different environments. Further generations develop differently, depending on where they happened to develop and grow. At what point the phospholipids and polymers are a living thing might be difficult to distinguish. The entity absorbs small molecules from the sea, incorporating various amino acids into its structure as it grows.

Suppose a cell in a human body is enlarged to the point where each proton is the size of a grain of salt, where there are 60 grains of salt to an inch. The cell would have grown to an incredible size, maybe as large as a small city. Organic chemistry has its own means of making partitions that function like walls, keeping one area separate from the next, opening channels between partitions, where particles flow to and from. The cell would also be in contact on all sides with other cells in the body. The whole point of the hypothetical enlargement is one can see that there is a plethora of activity in a very tiny space. Millions of atomic nuclei each 200 feet from the next, together making complex structures.

Life developing on planets orbiting stars among the 100 billion galaxies of the known universe, when one considers that other planets will have volcanic activity and lighter elements spewing out all over the surface some time after creation in supernova, would be inevitable. The second law of thermodynamics and the small size of individual atoms combines to create an increasing level of complexity among the lighter elements. These lead to living things, and in the entire universe that would have happened countless times.

Plant life, marine life, terrestrial life, and avian life would be found as life flourished in every available niche, employing various survival adaptations. Plants on other worlds would have appendages holding them stationary on land and underwater, and similarities here, too, could be inferred, roots and branches are the appendages of plants, and plant life elsewhere would also branch out in some way or another for nutrients. Marine life would develop a means of extracting oxygen from water, flying creatures would develop ultra-light materials for wings and feathers, for the most part. Maybe in some instances gravity is stronger than here, and avian life fails because things can't fly fast or long enough to evade capture by predators. At what specific gravity does avian life face certain failure as life develops on alien planets with liquid water, amino acids, etc., would be an intriguing question to answer.

Other guesses can be made about life on other planets. If the environment is a safe haven for multi-cellular life to take hold, it probably will. Once that has begun, survival of the fittest will leave creatures that survive only. Development of sense organs, appendages, and central nervous system happened here as battles for survival among animals with movement raged, and those same attributes would probably be common among living creatures capable of movement on other planets.

A head and eyes and ears could be a lot more commonplace than one might think. A mouth with taste buds, some kind of olfactory organ, and all these kinds of original developments could be based on the need to adapt and evolve, like here.

The same kind of things that course through our atmosphere, course through alien atmospheres. Light waves in various spectra, sound waves of varying lengths and intensity, odors of various things, would be as abundant there as here. Eyes, ears, and nose had better get developed or living creatures go extinct. Eventually some creature succeeds and reproduces. After a million years many different species are found, all with the common ancestor that successfully developed the sense organs to survive at a more primitive level.

In this hypothetical alien world it is now hard to find an animal that does not have the survival equipment of various sense organs, a brain and nervous system, and four appendages. Quite likely some 6 and 8 legged creatures will develop, and just like here, be smaller creatures than the four legged ones. As on Earth four legged creatures in the alien world would have, on the appendages nearest the brain, special adaptations to help the creature possessing them to capture prey, break open seeds, and whatever other manipulative activity. One of the more adept would gain the position of apex creature.

Plants on other planets would in some cases produce fruit that is edible for animals but also propagate the plant species, and poisonous fruit would probably develop among some species. The DNA molecule has some very close relatives. All the chemical changes going on, like oxidation, erosion, photosynthesis, are as equally likely on far distant planets.

Here on Earth, there is around 21% oxygen. Why this should be so wasn't clear until not too many years ago. If the percentage of oxygen in the atmosphere rises, fire burns more readily. Were an excess of oxygen to occur, forest fires would start more readily, and quickly consume the excess oxygen and levels in the air would fall back again to around 21%. A similar type of constraint on the levels of oxygen would be found on other worlds as well.

Naturally we are curious about other life in the universe, actually meeting other intelligent beings is another thing. The distances to other stars are huge, and the time and travel long and dangerous. It could happen, but even if it doesn't, we could rest easy in the certainty that life would have gotten started on other planets as well, and some of these living things would develop intelligence.

Chances are an intelligent life form developed a real long time ago. Recent estimates based on stellar evolution, and relative abundances of metals in stars distant conclude that life on planets such as ours likely didn't become possible until the known universe had reached 10 billion years after the Big Bang. One could hypothesize ancient aliens capable of hopping from one system of galaxies to another, and though unlikely, a civilization trillions of years old is theoretically possible. If we are ever visited by aliens, it will be by exploring, curious beings that would attempt to communicate. They would have developed culture and explored the sciences, just like us, but for a far longer time. Technology to translate alien languages might in time be possible, just based on how fast computer processors are doubling in speed in our civilization. Expect aliens

No contact when the species is not in control of its environment

to understand us if they made it this far, and we can expect to understand them when they try to communicate due to greater computer abilities in the future. At the very least, the aliens would be able to say something using one of our languages in printed word form, maybe even have a machine that could make sounds necessary to communicate with speech.

The aliens would have had more opportunity to study our language, as they approached the Earth, than we would have been able to study theirs, if an alien species were to ever make contact. The aliens would likely send radio transmissions in one of the major languages of Earth after listening to us a while. We wouldn't need to know their language, though it would eventually be translated if we became friends with the aliens. I like to think it possible, maybe someday happen that we do truly meet alien travelers, a first time for everything.

Any contact by intelligent species would be minimal because of possible contamination. They would be wary of corrupting life support on the vessel they travel in. Just opening a spacecraft door on Earth could bring in enough molds and spores to completely overcome the living things within, depending on what eats what, something not easy to answer until it happens.

Collecting specimens from Earth would be done secretly, to lower the risk of problems. They would not involve us since that would complicate a simple extraction that would not harm us materially. Any contact between life forms on one planet and life forms from another planet could have any number of unknown consequences, most of which we would be unable to predict. Molds and spores are just the first on a long list. Foreign DNA ingested by local animals or plants could begin changes we could only guess at. Viruses that are dormant within visiting beings could run rampant within us, or vice versa. Intestinal bacteria could switch species. Different enzymes from food from another planet might start some chemical processes difficult to predict.

We have to assume that most life would be very similar to life on Earth, but small differences on the scale of cells and DNA could still make food from another planet risky. Of all of the dangers of space travel, the inability to find food on other planets that is safe to eat may be the one that dooms most space travel attempts. A space craft with no living survivors could drift by, the travelers having starved to death a million years before.

An alien species if visiting Earth might take samples quietly, do some testing on animal and plant matter, and decide if the organisms on Earth are compatible with them. If they were to decide the Earth was a habitable biosphere for them, they might then make contact. That this hasn't happened indicates we haven't been visited, or the aliens saw the life forms here were incompatible, and left.

The best chance for alien life to begin to inhabit an alien world would be finding a planet that was very early in the development of life, similar to how the Earth was 4 billion years ago. Older civilizations would have advanced astronomy and probably be able to single out such planets, especially if the civilization had been around long enough to witness numerous supernova nearby. Seeding of the planet with plant life of the primitive type, and microbial life from the home world, and a wait of a few thousand years might make it inhabitable. The home world DNA, or equivalent, would traverse the oceans of the new world, and be found in all life forms. The aliens might then safely move there, bringing more advanced life with them.

The UFO business is booming, and even to me it seems that our airplanes may have been buzzed by advanced craft. The only business in UFO's consists in making fantasy movies there from. There is no tangible evidence of any matter from some other solar system, or alien bodies. The UFO craze is entertainment.

With all the difficulties of maintaining a space craft in operating condition over long periods of time, the difficulty of finding anything suitable to eat on alien planets, and aggression on the part of inhabitants of alien planets suggests that finding young planets and seeding them with home world DNA would be best suited to an intelligent species.

That species could be nearing the end of the life of the star in its home world, or face some other disaster that looms, and the chances of moving to some other world uninhabited by intelligent beings would be a whole lot safer than making targets of themselves near planets like ours, with the chance of being met with aggression, or a refusal to share the Earth with them.

Earth is doomed, and you have two spacecraft to choose from, one traveling to a planet with some intelligent beings, the other to a planet with no intelligent life, seeded with home world DNA of various forms. Without question the planet that has no intelligent life yet, populated with home world DNA throughout, would be the best choice.

Curious that if intelligent species developed

elsewhere in the universe, and this truly has happened, they would have developed on a planet with liquid water in all probability, and liquid water on the surface there would have evaporated and joined the air, just as here, and one could say that these intelligent aliens also have had some experience with weather phenomenon.

Intelligent aliens would have also noticed that copper, or anything that conducts electricity well, and lead or any non-conducting material in pure form of some specific quantity in an elevated location can cause changes in barometric pressure, and precipitation amounts, at some time in their development as intelligent beings. Weather could prove to be the most discussed topic in the entire known universe, not just Earth. It would be impossible presently to take a survey, though.

Our best hope to find intelligent life in the universe would probably be through radio signals than real contact. If one day we translate a transmission from afar, we would then respond, after which a wait of a century, maybe even 1000 years or more might be needed for a return message. SETI, the search for extraterrestrial intelligence, has thus far failed to find a signal, but it someday should happen.

The current estimate of stars in the Milky Way is as many as 400 billion; the number of planets at least equal to that. If only one in 100 planets have liquid water, there would be at least 4 billion planets where life could develop in our galaxy. Our Sun alone has contributed two such planets.

Chapter 4.Weather Modification

Such an opportunity exists; perception of it is lacking
JB

Nikola Tesla had ideas about providing abundant water to dry areas, controlling flooding and other weather control ideas. These ideas, and many others, were never developed by him. Those familiar with Tesla know that he was a prolific inventor with numerous inventions and patents, and his finances fluctuated wildly. A method of modifying the weather would not likely have yielded a weekly paycheck for him, whereas a number of other ideas he had offered a better chance of financial returns. Not to say that Tesla himself thought it through like that, more likely he just pursued various things as he saw fit, such as building an alternating current motor. What struck him as he pondered his ideas is probably lost to us for all time, what we do have is all his unfinished business.

Tesla voided his contract with Westinghouse on his alternating current invention, which paved the way for Westinghouse Electric to be able to afford to switch over to alternating current from direct current in use, championed by Edison, but inferior to alternating current. Whatever his thoughts and decisions were, we are still blessed by many things that Nikola Tesla invented and developed. Maybe we should add one more. It has been claimed that some agency of the U.S. Government seized Tesla's private papers upon his demise.

Charles Hatfield came along in the early part of the 20th century, sometime around 1900 or so, and was known to claim to be able to make it rain. A meteorology text where I learned of this man stated that he was paid by the mayors of a number of towns and cities to work his mysterious cure for drought stricken areas. The book also mentions that he seemed to be successful in his attempts. The places where he was hired to do this did see rain soon after he was hired and did his thing.

What Hatfield did was burn some copper compounds in a pyre type furnace, copper sulfide or sulfate, releasing plumes of copper compounds that rose into the atmosphere and joined the gases and dust that was there and began to follow the prevailing westerlies just as the rest of the gases and dust do. He also claimed different secret ingredients went into the concoction he burned. Seems Hatfield himself was not anxious to reveal what he was doing, maybe because it was simple.

The author of the meteorological text I had perused regarded this Charles Hatfield as a sort of charlatan. In the opinion of the author these copper compounds that Hatfield sent airborne didn't really have any effect on the weather. He went on to state similar claims had been made about the presence of some metal or other making an impact upon the weather, and said these were all just wishful thinking, with no basis in fact.

That was that, apparently, one paragraph in a book with part of the title "Weather Modification" copyright 1980, some 400 pages in length. I never read the entire book, but I find myself wondering what the author could have possibly filled it with, since all that changes the weather, according to meteorologists, is cloud seeding, and that only a little. I found it peculiar that someone would write a book about a subject that according to the author and his peers, has so little subject matter. I looked up the title since I couldn't remember the author's name and found three books that could have been the one that I looked through and found that one paragraph and the mention of Blue Nile. These three possibilities are listed in the references at the end of the book, all copyright 1980.[7]

That is apparently how things currently stand with regard to the subject of this book. The three authors must have known the water molecule would be likely, as water vapor, to be responsive to an external electrical field such as would be created by a row of copper tubing in a high location. Yet one of the authors states otherwise.

Blue Nile, or Nile Blue was a military research program classified in 1945, and according to the author of the book I had looked through, was still classified as of 1980. Recently a program aired about military weather modification activity where the trail in Vietnam used by the North to infiltrate the South was in the 60's cloud seeded by the U.S. military, and this activity appeared to flood out the trail as often as not, and this was what Blue Nile was, according to the presentation.

What little I know of chem-trails, is that some thing is added to jet fuel, or something is added to the exhaust as it exits the engine and depending on what those chemicals are, this activity could create a path of least resistance. The similarity to this weather modification activity and what Hatfield did are apparent. Hatfield, on the ground, in a high location, sent chemical compounds to the air in a furnace, with the rising heated air ferrying the compounds upwards to clouds.

The height at which the jet that releases tainted exhaust could vary, but flying through the air at any height is a pretty good release point for a chemical that could prove to be an effective ingredient in modifying the weather. In comparison, chem-trails seem more direct and perhaps more effective.

With ground based and air delivered exhausts, whether from a furnace or a jet, a great number of tiny particulates are released airborne that water molecules can latch on to and begin accumulating into raindrops, and if the molecules happen to also create a path of least resistance, there is the certainty that barometric pressure will fall, and clouds will begin developing. The developing clouds and the particulates ready to start raindrops might work together well.

However, one would have to consider the costs of being without whatever chemicals are burned each time, since once the chemicals are sent airborne the chances of being able to recover the material is non-existent. Pure copper placements could always be adjusted in quantities to accommodate the creation of storms of the desired size, and, given safeguards against theft, always remain in the possession of the weather modifier.

The earliest smelters of metals could have picked up on this back in the bronze age. It would be interesting to see if some translations of ancient writings have been wrongly interpreted and actually refer to rainfall and metals. The irrigation was extensive in Roman and Mayan cities, and maybe they knew they could depend on rain happening. The early smelters of metals hadn't yet separated copper from zinc. What they got was a combination of the two metals. Bronze conducts electricity as well, probably slightly less conductive than pure copper. By the time of the Roman Empire copper may have been purified, the Mayans maybe not.

Suppose the ancient smelters of bronze had an open pit mine some ways up a hillside. They find a vein of metal ore, hack at it and shovel it out. They dig a pit near the spot, to burn the ore and purify the metal. Ancient sites have evidence that this was the typical procedure. They had no trucks or bulldozers, no easy way to move the ore. They worked it near the mine they hacked it out of.

After a day of smelting a weight of bronze ingots piles up off to the side of the fire pit. After about the fourth day, once the fire started, it started raining, so the fire went out. The crew then began to transport the bronze ingots down the hillside to the town. Finishing that, they waited a day for the rain to stop. Then they climbed back up the hill and after a few days of digging, got the fire going again and began to produce more bronze ingots.

Fourth day into the smelting it starts raining again. Ingots piling up on the side of the fire pit. This happens almost a whole summer until one time when it started raining they didn't bring the ingots down the hill because there were festivities in the town under the big tent. This time the rain doesn't stop, but continues for almost three days.

The crew leader after three days sends the crew up the muddy hill to retrieve the ingots. After the rain stops the crew goes back up the hill and starts digging out more ore and get the fire going again. Then, the crew leader brings a couple young boys from town along once the fire gets going, and they transport the ingots down the hill to the town as soon as they get a cart full. Rain doesn't happen on the fourth day, and the crew leader isn't surprised. He explains to his boss the bronze on the hillside seemed to make it rain, it usually took about 72 hours after some ingots had been cast and left on the hillside and the rulers of Rome find out.

A not impossible scenario such as that could have occurred in the Roman empire and in South America with the Mayans. Probably in each instance only the nobility would have learned of this, had the process been noticed back then.

Those giving directions on how to build irrigation canals wouldn't have shared the insight with lesser citizens, and when those civilizations fell this knowledge would have been long forgotten, those once aware of it long dead. Bronze or copper, it wouldn't have mattered. What mattered was did anyone notice that the ingots piling up on the hill made a difference in frequency of rainfall.

Due consideration has to be given to what was happening in those two empires, and what brought on the development of extensive irrigation canals in both. Maybe Romans and Mayans both simply liked adorning settlements with bronze sculptures once bronze smelting was well underway, and numerous bronze sculptures were scattered around the hilly terrain that a lot of both empires rested on. That fact, indeed, may have been the source of the precipitation that eventually inspired the building of intricate irrigation systems as time progressed. Inhabitants could have been blissfully unaware that the bronze smelting and the bronze sculptures around the cities could have had something to do with the precipitation. The decline of the Mayan Empire could have been partly due to the weather, with frequent hurricanes and heavy flooding.

The atmosphere on Earth is comprised of vast numbers of sub-microscopic gases which have been fairly well described; about 78% nitrogen, 21% oxygen, a little argon and tiny amounts of carbon dioxide, methane and a few other gases. Also in the air is water vapor in varying amounts, sunlight, static electricity, dust, and impossibly small primordial specks as before mentioned.

All of the particles mentioned, not including static electricity or sunlight, are small satellites in orbit around the Earth in the same manner that the Moon is a satellite in orbit around the Earth.

The difference in size is pronounced, though, and that difference results in the orbits of all these tiny satellites being very easily perturbed by all the neighboring satellites. These satellites that comprise the atmosphere are also much closer to the Earth than the Moon, so the uneven terrain of the Earth also factors into how easily and often these satellites are perturbed in their orbits.

Laws of inertia hold that an object in motion tends to stay in motion. This holds true even for the tiniest things. The fact that the orbits of these atmospheric objects are easily altered doesn't change the fact that in the absence of anything causing them to alter course these objects would proceed in an orbit around the Earth similar to that of the Moon, though the moon doesn't follow the prevailing westerlies. The ease by which the air components can be made to alter course is evident.

The magnetic field of the Earth varies at different locations around the globe such as the magnetic pole and this can alter the orbits of our atmospheric satellites. The Moon is responsible, along with the

Sun, for creating ocean tides, and changing tides also have an influence on some of the air. The Jet Stream has an impact on the flow of the air.

Every moving object on land, or sea, or in the air changes some of the orbits of some of the Earth's atmosphere. I wave my hand, a whale breaches off the coast of Alaska, a jet plane flies from San Diego to New York, etc., the movements of all these different things send atmospheric constituents scattering. As the Earth spins on its axis, the air is pulled along with the rotating Earth.

Hence we have winds that are known as the prevailing westerlies. These winds blow from west to east almost everywhere around the planet. At or near the poles these winds are not as clearly defined since the top and bottom of our spinning planet doesn't travel as far in a day's revolution as the land areas away from the poles.

Standing at the North Pole every direction is south, so there are no prevailing westerlies. Equally true of the South Pole, every direction is north from there. The winds likely have varying patterns over the poles. One could stand at one of the poles and know the Eastern Hemisphere is on one's left, and the Western Hemisphere is on one's right, so there is a kind of west and east at the poles.

It is held that gravitational and electromagnetic forces are a wave phenomenon. All matter exerts forces gravitational and electromagnetic. These forces are invisible. They are both thought to be different aspects of the single wave that all matter propagates at the speed of light equally in all directions. These forces weaken with distance. Gravity is quite weaker than electromagnetism, as mentioned earlier. The gravitational field of the

Earth is strong because the Earth is huge, and aircraft need lots of energy to escape this field.

This wave propagating from matter is difficult to understand since it is only detectable when a large quantity of matter together exerts a force, such as the Earth's magnetic fields.

One atom alone emitting these waves isn't detectable, as far as I know, since detecting a single atom by itself is just barely possible, and the wave there from must be faint indeed. Only able to observe effects in the aggregate, with quantities of matter showing the only observable phenomena, limits one's capacity to perceive what is really happening within the individual atoms. That is the reason the mechanisms of gravity are not fully known.

Copper is an element known for its capacity to conduct electricity. It conducts electricity so well because copper atoms together in some copper naturally arrange themselves in orderly rows. When an electrical current encounters a group of copper atoms, it passes between the atoms at nearly the speed of light, with little friction in its passage. As with all matter, copper also sends out electromagnetic waves at the speed of light.

Tiny air molecules, static electricity, dust, primordial specks, water molecules and anything else airborne in the vicinity of a quantity of copper will encounter the neat, orderly kind of arrangement that copper exhibits. All of these airborne objects would encounter less friction near the copper. A path of least resistance would exist in the vicinity of this quantity of copper, a path which tiny, free floating entities would flow more easily along than any other direction.

Water molecules will align themselves along the path of least resistance. Copper as stable isotopes has a net positive charge. With a positive charge to the copper tubing, the negatively charged oxygen atom in each water molecule would align toward the copper, and begin to move that way. Water molecules from hundreds of miles away could begin herding to the location of the copper placement.

This no doubt explains why Charles Hatfield appeared to have been successful in his efforts, and why the Tesla coil experiments saw intense thunderstorms. The copper compounds sent airborne, the copper Tesla coils on the platform in Colorado Springs, must each have created a path of least resistance along which water molecules and primordial specks began to flow.

Once the process began, barometric pressure would fall as all objects in the air are traveling in the same direction, encountering each other less frequently since two or more things traveling in the same direction will not meet. The electrically inert of the atmospheric components are pulled along gravitationally with the water molecules and primordial specks.

That is the essence of the matter, the fact that two or more things traveling in the same direction do not meet. Barometric pressure is a measure of the degree to which objects in the air are meeting each other. A high barometric pressure reading indicates that the air at that point in time is going through more chaotic behavior, with interactions between air molecules happening more frequently. A lower barometric pressure reading indicates air molecules are “schooling”, moving in unison, large numbers of atmospheric particles traveling in the same general direction and interacting between themselves less frequently.

I think most people realize the atoms of things don't really touch each other; they come close, but the field surrounding the nucleus, created by the electrons, is strong enough to preclude other atoms from entering. A bullet that was fired into a tree trunk blasted into the wood, and penetrated several inches, but not a single atom touched any other one. The individual atoms remained sealed within that protective boundary provided by the tightly orbiting electrons.

Atoms seem to touch during fusion. In nuclear fusion, when hydrogen, or deuterium atom nuclei join, and become one nucleus, one hydrogen nucleus or deuterium nucleus had to get past the electron of the other. The higher up the table of elements one goes, the heavier the nucleus of the element. A nucleus with many protons combining with another would involve close contact.

Gases differ from solid objects. Gases deflect off each other a lot but don't really touch. How much that is happening is where air pressure rises or falls. The hotter gases are, the more excited they become, raising air pressure. Land heats up faster than water, so the faster heating also adds to raising air pressure on land by day.

The dark matter and energy would be charged and definitely school because of a conductive metal of sufficient size being in a high location in an area, and the N_2 and O_2 would have no choice but to follow a stream of things traveling in one direction many times more massive than itself.

It is likely the dark matter and dark energy are charged particles. The known particles that are electrically inert have gone through a number of changes, first becoming hydrogen, then helium, then eventually nitrogen or oxygen, then pairing up with a like atom before they reach the state of being electrically inert. Single oxygen atoms are a charged entity, but they do not stay single for long because oxygen reacts readily with other atoms, including other single oxygen atoms.

The unknown particles are likely fragments trying to join with others of its kind, so they are unlikely so complete as to be inert and uninfluenced by the electromagnetic waves emanating from the copper placement in the hypothetical weather experiment. Magnetic monopoles as small as these primordial specks must be would satisfy the theory. One also wonders whether the smallness of dark matter and dark energy wouldn't of itself be enough to make them, if they are indeed magnetic monopoles, react to the electromagnetic force of the copper.

Burning copper compounds results in a loss of scarce material, and since the same effect could be expected with placement of a quantity of copper, 500 to 1000lbs., in as high a location as possible, that means would be the most economical to apply.

My estimate is that somewhere from 500 to 1000lbs. would be a sufficient quantity, one that could be retrieved and used over without loss of material. Some differences would have to be expected at different locations around the world since some places are closer to an ocean than others, some have very uneven terrain, etc.

Precipitation will usually occur around seventy two hours after placement of copper in a high location. Close to an ocean to the west would reduce time and quantity needed considerably, while in the middle of the Gobi Desert the elapsed time required before precipitation occurred could be hours longer, and require twice as much copper. Quantity needed to see the desired amounts of rainfall could vary considerably around the world, but even the desert in Chile on a high plateau could see rainfall with a large quantity of copper situated advantageously. In that very high location, 1200 pounds of copper might be needed.

This desert would be a great place to start for a group of scientists to confirm the hypothesis, since at the top of the plateau it almost never rains. If an experiment were tried there and rain occurred around 72 hours later the idea of coincidence could be ruled out. Especially if, once that happened and the experimenters packed up, left, and the desert returned to a dry condition, and upon returning a month later, upon again attempting the same type experiment, rain came again around 72 hours later.

The surface area of hollow copper tubing being greater than solid bars of copper, hollow circular tubing would produce a more dramatic effect than bars of solid copper. If the copper is on a horizontal plane, a robust wind will develop; if placed on an upward slope or vertically, there is less wind and more cumulonimbus type cloud development, and precipitation is more robust.

The idea is to take coils of copper tubing, two feet in diameter, and arrange those in six foot tall circular things resembling a bird cage without a top or bottom. A number of six foot long straight bars of copper tubing could be used as supports, tied to the circular tubing with copper wire. Stand the six foot tall copper coil objects on end so they stand straight up, and since this will require a half dozen or more of these contraptions, place them in a row from the west to the east, with a slight curve towards north, to help to create counterclockwise wind flow.

If you are in the southern hemisphere, low pressure systems spin clockwise down there. Therefore a row of copper coil placements in the southern hemisphere would probably work best if it began from the west and worked to the east curving slightly south. In either hemisphere, an upward slope on the western side of a mountain or hill would work best.

After two days the sky will be pretty much cloud covered in its entirety. From the second day on, rain could occur at any time, depending on when night falls, but will occur by the end of three days, perhaps 8 hours longer. If the copper is removed, the effect remains for a few days to a week with lessening intensity, the effect of inertia.

Trying to see what would happen if one brought an 800 pound block of solid copper and put it on a hilltop, I really don't know what would happen. I assume that it occupying a smaller space might be likely to lessen the impact it might have. It would surely have an impact. The density of the material might make this type of weather modification more intense, for all I know. Until someone tries such an experiment with a solid block of copper instead of copper coils and presents the results to the public, the actual difference is unknown. Solid blocks are more difficult to transport. The primary part of the whole concept is the enormous size of a quantity of copper in comparison to the size of single atoms or small molecules and fragments remaining from the Big Bang. The naturally occurring conductivity of pure copper in a high location makes an impact, dependent upon how much copper is positioned.

The arrangement of circular coils standing on end and spread out ten feet apart as described can be done by just about anyone, or several people, almost anywhere. Some of the terrain on Earth is harder to travel than other places, especially near the tops of mountains. If one could drive a truck to 7000 feet above sea level, on the western side of a 9000 feet above sea level mountain, chances are that parking the truck and deploying the copper there would work.

No need to haul the material any further than one needs to position it usefully. Find an upward slope and create a row of the things, from west to east, sloping up and curving north in the northern hemisphere, and curving south down under.

600 pounds. 5 days up, 8 days down, until further notice.

I have seen the observation made that rules that apply to ordinary things, or other disciplines in the natural sciences besides meteorology, don't apply to meteorology because the atmosphere is too complex on the Earth. Chaos theory applies. It is a vast system with a number of unique land and water features; The Grand Canyon, The Dead Sea, huge deserts, rain forests, and oceans. The quantity of air molecules is huge. No two storms are identical.

These features are no cloak for meteorologists to hide behind in a concerted effort to avoid facing this issue. If a predictable amount of rainfall occurs when a quantity of copper is experimented with as I've described, and if that quantity of copper being redeployed does essentially the same thing a second time it wouldn't matter that there were differences in the rainfall totals between adjacent counties in the area, or that the center of the storm front was 20 miles more north than the previous experiment, or that one storm front moved due east, and the next one took a more northeasterly direction.

The results would still be within the parameters of the theory, and definitive conclusions could be made, allowing for some variations between the individual storms. Suppose an experiment using copper is tried when the current forecast calls for no clouds for four days with a few high clouds expected to roll in on the fifth day. A pair of helicopters sweeps the area in advance for 500 miles in every direction for unusual barometric readings, declares the area clear, and the copper is placed in its location. A result consistent with the theory occurs, rain began around 9 P.M., 68 hours after the start of the experiment, a small storm with about a half inch of precipitation.

A week later a location is found 600 miles distant with a forecast for cloudless skies for a week. The crew choppers to the new site, which is then swept barometrically, and within hours of learning of the forecast have the new experiment going. 71 hours later precipitation begins, a similar storm system of the previous one. Eventually a decision that the process is true and valid must be reached.

Chaos theory predicts that if a system of things exceeds a certain level of complexity, predictions about expected events within that system are impossible. Yet if we can reliably predict the outcome of atmospheric events 72 hours into the future, this holding true within certain parameters in every instance the experiment is tried, provided that is what happens, we have proven otherwise. Not only that we have also proven that a cause and effect relationship does exist between a placement of copper on a mountain side or other high location, and an atmospheric event, rain, occurring around 72 hours after the start of an experiment with copper in a high location. Once the essential mechanism has been isolated, the specific quantities of copper required at various locations could be ascertained.

Clouds block sunlight. Additional precipitation on land means increased clouds over land. Such clouds would be much more effective at helping reduce worldwide temperatures than the cloud generation over the oceans proposed by the Discovery Channel Project Earth Program. The generation of additional clouds over land where things heat up faster than water, things like concrete and asphalt, would be more effective than cloud development over the oceans where the water stays cool, and the added clouds could contribute to hurricane development, especially since humanity has not yet implemented this proposed solution. For that to happen the process would need to be entered in encyclopedia.

Where a quantity of copper is resting can be important. A mountaintop, one would think, would be the best location. Placing the copper a hundred feet or so from the summit of a mountain, on the west side, could prove more effective in helping a storm front to develop. The difference in pressure between the west side of the hill where the copper rests and the east side which is blocked from the electromagnetic signal of the copper could be pronounced enough to create a front line between the two air masses that develop.

Places on Earth that ordinarily receive ample amounts of rain might begin to see less when drier places begin to take in more water, such as the Amazon or Indonesia or the Hawaiian Islands. If the residents of these areas are aware of what is taking place and are aware that they are free to remedy the situation they are having for themselves no problem exists. There appears to be more than enough total water vapor evaporating daily to satisfy every acre of land on the planet.

The oceans would see less precipitation than normal if much more water vapor than usual were diverted toward land, so island chains would be affected. If the island residents are unaware that the weather is being modified in some areas of the world and are also unaware that they, too, could change the weather, then there is a problem. When all residents of Earth can learn these things in an encyclopedia, there would be little doubt that should the need arise, steps could be taken to increase or decrease precipitation as needed, on a local basis. Doesn't seem likely that increased weather modification activities as described, copper high up, would turn Earth into a Water

World, like the movie of a few years ago. The hydrogen would be coming into existence anyway around the globe, and where a human act of weather modification was causing more hydrogen to be created, at the same time in the oceans hydrogen synthesis would slow down as a result of the precursors to hydrogen having gone elsewhere, namely to follow the path of least resistance created by the weather modification activities. The total hydrogen coming into existence on the Earth probably wouldn't change, so the amount of water on the Earth would be unaffected.

The Earth loses some of the atmosphere to outer space all the time, including water vapor, and the total quantity appears to be fairly stable. Here we could have the main reason that global warming is becoming a problem. If some hydrogen comes to exist daily to combine with oxygen to make a ton of water, then the Earth is gaining water daily. Measuring the total of water molecules on Earth might be very difficult. As noted, two tons of water is only 500 gallons, an amount that would go unnoticed on a daily basis spread among all the oceans. After a very long time the Earth may have more water but if that happens it probably would with or without human activity, and be a result of hydrogen being made in the universe that we haven't changed, except to increase such activity in some areas while decreasing that activity in other areas on the planet.

Crop yields would see an enormous boost from the lack of severe weather and the abundance of fresh water around the Earth. Plants prefer certain environments. The litchi tree requires a place with as little wind as possible since the litchi fruit are so easily dislodged by the wind, and conditions like that could be made to happen in some areas. Rain totals could be increased in spring and summer, and reduced in the fall for harvesting. Too often crops have matured and been destroyed by unwanted rain in September or October. This type of misfortune can easily be averted.

Thunder and lightning are usually more prevalent and the lightning more likely to strike the target when a quantity of copper tubing is placed in a vertical position on a mountain top or building roof. A lightning strike could be captured by a copper scaffolding arranged so that when lightning struck it, the electricity would travel along the copper down to an underground circle of some super conducting material of considerable size where it could circle at the speed of light. Hopefully, room temperature super conducting materials will be developed in the not too distant future. That has been the subject of research for some time.

A few controls, some switches, and the power is sent to the national electrical grid. The scaffolding would have to be no bigger than what would cause medium sized storms in an area. An area that can handle lots of rain would be needed. A crew with a cherry picker would be needed to make repairs to the scaffold after damage from lightning strikes. A ship sturdy enough to stay afloat during intense storms could prowl the ocean with copper on deck, or a platform like an oil rig could be constructed at sea, far from frequently used shipping lanes.

If such an attempt to catch electricity is made, there is a possibility that if the copper scaffolding is large enough it may even be able to channel and collect ambient static electricity in the surrounding air and generate some power without lightning striking the device, though this would be a lot less than three million volts, the average voltage of a lightning blast. But there are small and big lightning bolts, so some may exceed 5 million volts while smaller ones are only a million volts or less.

Hopefully a good percentage of a 3 million volt lightning blast would get captured by the storage ring, and doled out to the power grid. Once in place the only maintenance is the repair to lightning damaged parts. Identical sized parts could be used, and the damaged parts recycled.

Some insulation would be required for the underground part, or part of the hold of an oil rig type of experiment in remote seas, and the crew would need a secure location for at sea and on ground activities like this. To capture electricity out over the seas would require an electrical cable along the floor of the sea, and the impact on local climate would need to be factored in with any land based such experiments.

What is possible is that through examining this presentation eventually by enough people, and after some time for civilization to digest the new information, and new super conducting materials in production, maybe a group of investors with a team of physicists and engineers might have a go at it.

Computer simulations with programs that have inputted all the new information would probably give a physicist or engineer a good prediction of events surrounding a rig all alone in the South Pacific with a quantity of perfectly conducting materials in the hold and also part of the mast and rigging above the deck, or the climactic changes expected with a try at it on land, where one would need to prevent flooding.

Lightning is energy of the best quality if it could be captured. Coal, natural gas, oil, all need to be mined and refined before being stored and slowly used, but lightning needs only be captured, stored, and sent to wherever needed. Nuclear power is the more dangerous and complex of any energy source.

A small arrangement for a local region to gather the desired quantities of water by placement of copper could be arranged. The same quantity of copper could be connected to a storage ring should lightning strike, and the likelihood of that would be pretty good, considering the conductivity of the copper and its height. Add a ground wire on top.

Near the top of Mount Wherever a cave is excavated, or an existing cave modified, and a storage ring housed within. At the entrance, two sided slabs are mounted on wheels to serve as a door; one side has a coat of lead, and that side is exposed to the atmosphere when the rain making device is inactive, and the other side is coated in copper. When rain is desired, the doors slide open, exposing the copper side to the air, while the Tesla Coil type copper is wheeled out onto the hillside.

After desired precipitation amounts are obtained, the rain making coil is rolled back in, the doors are closed, and the copper is no longer exposed, but rather the lead exposure begins to raise the air pressure, or at the least, stop the electromagnetic waves of the copper. The coils suffered several lightning strikes, and are repaired in the safety of the cave, behind the lead shield.

The electricity from lightning helps the world convert more quickly to electric cars. Worldwide, five hundred such devices could fit comfortably, perhaps more. The whole process of putting things like that together would take a long time. Every island chain in the oceans would eventually have one. The only maintenance would be repair or replacement of the parts damaged by lightning.

A steady condition of a large quantity of copper being sat in place indefinitely in the highest available location will yield a storm front every 3 to 4 days. Once the storm comes through a cold front with winds from a northern or opposite direction of the storm will blow for a day or so followed by renewed cloud accumulation and the winds swinging back to originate in the southwest, or northwest, depending on which hemisphere the experiment is in.

This cold front that follows a precipitation event, after some hours of rain, is an important cooling factor. The more times a placement of copper on high produces a storm front over land, one can also count on the cooling effect of the cold front that follows, and all the clouds that develop during the storm development that are also cooling influences over land during the daytime.

Leaving it in place may see a lessening in strength as nature accustoms itself to the new feature in the landscape; removing the copper for a week every two months or adding a few hundred pounds after a few months to bring precipitation yields back to desired levels might be needed. The sudden change, when copper in quantity is first placed somewhere, will always be more dramatic than something in permanent position. Winds will show a marked preference for the direction of a row of copper tubing.

The jet stream will align to the row of copper. An acquaintance once said he saw an article in a mechanical magazine where they discussed using rows of copper at airports to assure that planes landing or taking off are facing a headwind rather than no wind or a tailwind.

Tornadoes and hail are problems that could be improved upon. There is considerable variation in the kinds of arrangements whereby copper tubing can be usefully positioned; all different kinds of experiments will be tried and each evaluated as to the effectiveness of reducing tornadoes, and hail.

For example, the litchi tree problem of needing as little wind as possible is probably solved by a slightly off vertical placement of copper, with a slight angle from the base to the top toward the west of about 20 degrees. The wind obeys the prevailing westerlies and at the same time the force of the westward slanted copper opposes the wind, causing a lull in the wind. One would need to try different angles to the copper and observe the effects, until the best angle reveals itself.

Farmers who grow litchis are well aware of the damage wind can do to the growth and ripening of the fruit, since the fruit won't grow if it has fallen off the tree. Most litchi farming is done in valley areas. The valley below the copper would see even less wind than the westward slanted copper in a higher location nearby.

The arrangement that would bring an end to the "Tornado Alley" in the middle of the U.S. each spring and summer could be more rain in the desert southwest and large copper arrangements near the north pole each spring and summer that would reduce the amount left to the great plains. It could take more than that to quiet down the tornado activity in the U.S., such as the entire world being intent upon an adequate supply of water, leaving any area not managed by humans subject to drought.

The middle of the United States may eventually need to use some copper in a high location to see any rain at all. When that situation arises the best solution to tornadoes will present itself, probably the use of numerous small amounts of copper that would yield rain but not huge storms. Maybe when rain is desired, there could be a double front moving across the country, one north, one south, with the jet stream split in two, weakening storms.

Usually what happens with tornadoes is huge storm cells seem to develop out of thunderstorms, and these sudden buildups are hard to predict. A copper placement where the angle was more to the horizontal with the wind, would cause winds to be robust enough to keep a storm front moving without stalling and accumulating into huge cells, still yielding rainfall, but not tornadoes.

Perhaps a multiple copper placement could be put to use in the entire area, four to eight different locations spread several hundred miles apart, which together with helping more wind prevent tornadoes, also assured that individual storms are decentralized enough. Unfortunately, trying different experiments with small amounts of copper in multiple locations would be difficult for one individual to do. With eight different locations with around 400 pounds of copper each spread from Wyoming to Alabama one might not get huge cumulonimbus clouds, but more generalized cloudiness and rain without tornadoes and hail. When cumulonimbus clouds start to look threatening, several rows of lead sheets might bring down the severity of upcoming storms considerably. The middle of the United States in spring needs rain, though. Quite a bit of agriculture goes on there. Trying to stop rain altogether with lead wouldn't do much either. No tornadoes replaced by drought.

The Polar Regions could be conduits for water vapor and static electricity on a yearly basis. A two ton row of copper in Northern Alaska might send enough weather toward the North Pole, leaving less in the middle of the U. S. Polar conditions being as they are, the logistics of placing copper tubing in a high location there is difficult, but not impossible.

Once some copper is positioned somewhere in the polar tundra exposed to the elements, it could be buried in snow and ice in three and a half days! A crew would have to visit occasionally and clear off the snow and ice, lest the copper is lost in a glacier.

A new cascade of low pressure starts by placing copper coils in circular stacks in a high location. An hour later, some small cumulonimbus clouds will begin to appear just east of and right above where the copper is resting. After eight hours puffy clouds will be appearing on all sides. At about twelve hours an additional cloud formation will begin to appear, surrounding the area where the copper is. This is a generalized hazy cloudiness, that thins the farther from the place where the copper is resting you go.

If the experiment began at 6AM, the first night wouldn't reveal much, but the next morning would show increased cumulonimbus clouds on all sides continuing to get thicker and larger, nearest the copper. Soon, any trace of the cause of the clouds would be hidden by overcast, as the cascade of lower pressure continues. If a path of least resistance exists where the copper is, it has an area where it is most intense. Schooling particles will be compressed closer together over time as the much higher pressure outside the area of the copper's most intense output exerts a push.

Copper will cause cloud streams

By dawn of the third day, around 72 hours after placing the copper in its location, rain will begin to fall. If it is during warm months thunderstorms would be likely. If the right quantity of copper is used, 6 to 12 hours of rain come and go, followed by a cold front, with winds blowing down from the north behind the low. Too much copper and rainfall is more intense, and lasts longer.

Leaving the copper in place, assuming the location is in the northern hemisphere, after a day or so of northeasterly winds and colder temperatures, the wind swings back to originate in the southwest, and cloud development begins anew. On the first day after the cold front, the probable location of the copper would be evident again from the area of generalized cloudiness, where the cumulonimbus clouds are most intense. The second day will again see complete overcast take over, and rain could begin a little sooner than the third day after the cold front, seven days into the copper being where it is.

This pattern would continue indefinitely, with occasional two day periods of steady rain, with an occasional break. If the area happened to be Lake Chad, and residents were intent upon refilling the lake, a choice to leave the copper more than a week or two might be made. Most often the copper would need to be brought closer to sea level and stored in a building, letting the area dry out.

Explaining all that might happen with copper and the atmosphere would take more experiment and observation than I have accumulated. There are many types of different arrangements one could try, yielding a slightly different result in each instance. One would have the topography of the Earth at any location, along with normal weather patterns in the area to consider. An experiment in one location on Earth repeated identically in some other location could yield quite different results. The only way to learn how much copper to position some place would be to conduct experiments and build a database containing as much detail about previous experiments as possible. Information such as distance from the nearest ocean, altitude of the copper, quantity of copper, how it is arranged on the hill, all these things would serve as a guide to future attempts. Disasters could be minimized.

One other thing that needs noting, when weather

modification activities are planned, is an escape plan. This applies to any attempt to modify the weather with copper. For instance, the county where you live decrees a weather emergency, rain is needed, and you and two other people are entrusted with placing some copper tubing in a high location previously chosen. You and your colleagues proceed to drive a truck loaded with copper to the agreed upon site.

For example, in the Las Vegas area, that could be Wheeler Pass, snaking up the west side of Mount Charleston. Once the truck leaves the Blue Diamond Highway, it is dirt road for twelve miles up the hill, with some hairpin turns and deep ruts.

You arrive at the chosen spot and deploy the copper as described by the meteorologist; three days later it starts raining heavily. You receive a phone call after 6 hours of hard rain to pack up the copper and return to town. The dirt road is a quagmire, all the dried up river beds are now active rivers. No hope of driving the truck down the dirt road with the rain as it is. With a situation just described, the copper would have to be taken away by helicopter, and that could be dangerous.

Thinking that one is in control of the weather, getting more rain than bargained for can happen, and without a means of getting the copper back down the hill, can lead to flooding, and ruin. Dirt roads and arroyos can change quickly with a lot of rain. Finding a location that is safer, from where one might depart safely should be a priority. Maybe that location isn't as elevated a position as the original, but would still work, maybe with slightly more copper than the higher location on the dirt road to get a similar result. If all one accomplishes is dangerous weather, damage to buildings, farms, there would be no point in doing it. Control is different from runaway disaster. When one is in control disaster doesn't happen. It is important that the exposure of the copper could be ended quickly, if needed, and returned to a building near sea level.

The start of the experiment begins with those entities in the atmosphere responsive to the electrical field of the quantity of copper in a high location beginning to proceed in that direction. The water molecules in the atmosphere, and the hypothesized primordial specks will begin to align themselves along the path of least resistance.

Relative humidity begins to rise. As more water molecules align themselves along the path of least resistance they exert increasing gravitational pull on the electrically inert atmospheric components.

Relative humidity is derived from humidity at the saturation point, which is 100% relative humidity, and the actual quantity at 30 degrees Celsius is 30 grams per cubic meter, a little over an ounce per kilogram of atmosphere. At 20 degrees Celsius the saturation point is around 15 grams per 1000 grams of atmosphere. The actual amount of water in the air is only 1.5% by weight at 68 degrees Fahrenheit, and yet, at that point, rain would develop. At this temperature, 7.5 grams of water per 1000 grams is 50% relative humidity, yet only 0.75 percent of the air by total weight is water molecules.

At the outset the distribution of primordial specks in the atmosphere is around ten times the mass and energy of the known atmosphere. If these entities were to increase in concentrations as well as the water molecule, the nitrogen and oxygen come along as these quantities of things traveling in the same direction grow during the experiment. What concentrations primordial specks reach could have no physical boundary beyond which it could accumulate further, as water molecules do. At 100% relative humidity, water molecules begin to condense out as precipitation, but primordial specks could still be increasing, and or more rapidly be becoming hydrogen or neutrons. However the two combine, together they are enough to pull the electrically inert nitrogen and oxygen along the path of least resistance. Thus, barometric pressure falls for the various reasons mentioned earlier, all airborne entities traveling in the same general direction. Water molecules are lighter than either paired isotope of nitrogen and oxygen, so 3% water by weight might be a higher percentage by volume, perhaps as much as 5 or 6%. Water by itself would rise and form clouds naturally after evaporation, being lighter than the nitrogen and oxygen isotopes.

Chapter 5. Public Concerns

Some things need doing frequently, but sparingly

JB

Man, acting in the social environment, competes with other men for scarce items of value. Having a competitive edge would go hand in hand with not sharing information that only you and maybe a few others possess. Anyone who happened to notice what copper can do to the atmosphere when it is placed on high could have decided not to speak to anyone about it. If anyone did say anything in the last century they would not have been believed anyway. There is ideological competition also. Anyone with a vested interest in keeping all of humanity ignorant of the weather modifying ability of recent discoveries would belittle the possibility.

There exist also politicians, for whom clarity is the most feared enemy of all. Any misinformation from some politician will gain the news, while the real news never reaches the public. The selective process that media companies employ side with the political views of those in power. What was meant to be a check upon unlimited power by government, the media, is currently anything but that. With all the competitive advantages knowing this process could involve, and with as much misinformation presented by news broadcasts, there exists also this almost deafening void where nothing much can be found about the processes described in this book. That leads me to the inescapable conclusion that a precedent was set in the early 20th century whereby meteorologists discounted any possible effects caused by a quantity of copper in a high location, and it has continued to this day.

There is a correlation between how much copper is placed near a mountaintop and how much rain occurs. One could deploy more copper than is necessary and cause flooding or tornadoes, possibly even hurricanes. Hence this discovery could be used as a weapon by anyone with other than honorable intentions. This could very well be the reason why no meteorological text contains information about this discovery. It is too easy to cause changes in the weather, changes that could be destructive in nature.

A ton of copper could leave three states under water in about four days. Never should anyone try such an experiment as we've described with that much copper, unless they are in the Gobi desert and have already tried a half ton with no success, or are trying to extinguish a forest fire. This is the moral high ground that the scientific community, the media, and the government are clinging to desperately, about to be swept away by the tides of progress, and the advancement of knowledge.

It is apparent the majority of meteorologists currently practicing that profession have never even heard of this possibility, except perhaps for one day, half asleep in a classroom, it was spoken of briefly and debunked. Some members of the meteorological community must have in the past been aware of this, and chose not to tell anyone what they had discovered. The same is true for people other than meteorologists. A few engineers surely learned this at some time, the early 20th century was the age of the engineer, and included three decades of wet weather, ending abruptly the spring following the Stock Market crash.

Besides copper having an impact upon the flow of air molecules, a non-conducting element such as lead would have the opposite effect, logically. Peace loving humans are already in possession of a means to counter attempts to disrupt peaceful weather conditions. At the first sign of possibly severe weather lead could be placed in a high location so as to bring about higher air pressure, and consequently, less severe weather.

In the United States there are barometric stations maintained all over the continent. When there is an unusual drop in barometric pressure in a given area,

we need to find that copper....

one that has not been planned, a helicopter search for the offending material could be conducted using a barometer, and readings could narrow the search area down to within a square mile or so. Since the material in search of would have to be in a high place to have any impact to begin with, chances are good that finding and removing any such unauthorized attempts to modify the weather involving copper in a high location could be accomplished, far before the seventy two hours needed for a storm front to fully develop. Every day people would need to be aware of the need to forward any changing weather information quickly.

In the event that someone were to burn some copper compounds after dark, Charles Hatfield style, using lead might be the only recourse, though spotting the source of these compound plumes could be accomplished, as when a sudden drop in barometric pressure sets in motion a search for a quantity of copper and none is found.

Where the barometric pressure readings were lowest would probably be fairly close to wherever the copper compounds went airborne. The area could be put under surveillance until next time the culprits attempt such a misdeed. Ideally, only licensed meteorologists with proper qualifications and permits would be legally conducting incursions into the weather in an area. Any other attempts by persons unknown should be considered an act of terrorism punishable by death. In contrast, now anyone with a pickup truck and access to enough copper (or lead) or the funds to pay for some could make life miserable for a lot of people.

Barometric pressure should soon begin to be watched more closely for unusual changes. Places that are prone to times when disastrous weather strikes should be prepared to position lead on high from time to time. This isn't something I ever did. However, the laws of physics are on my side. Extrapolating to what is likely to happen when lead is placed somewhere high up from what happens when copper is placed somewhere high up isn't impossible. Which metal is stronger of the two is anyone's guess. If placing lead high up has less of an impact than placing copper on high, a war between the two would see copper the victor.

The only way to find that out would be to begin some experiments in this regard. If it turns out flooding can't be stopped by placing lead high up, one would be forced to locate the offending copper and remove it. Negative electromagnets may repel water molecules, making any cloud development difficult, if not impossible. Positively charged electromagnets would attract water molecules, and any experiments with such electromagnets should also be carefully monitored. The heavens can open up with scads of precipitation off and on for weeks, and it can stop raining for months, both through human intervention. The intervention wouldn't be evident without a barometric search, though, and the difference between a naturally occurring event and one with an added metal deposit or electromagnet wouldn't be evident either, unless one knew what to look for.

A swift response coupled with a harsh penalty for such acts could make things safer than they are now. Hurricane Rita and the aftermath had some web sites that claimed the storm was a man made event, though there wasn't much elaboration as to how this was done or by whom. There was talk of electromagnetic pulse generation, such as the HAARP experiments. Here we are, unprepared for such acts in an era with such a thing as the world wide web, and satellites worldwide as well, all around Earth. A quantity of copper on a mountain top can be pinned down fairly accurately just by watching as the clouds develop. The area nearest the copper will have, in addition to some thicker clouds than the surrounding area, a misty, hazy cloud structure covering a one to five mile circle. Farther out, the clouds will turn into thin streams, all seeming to drift toward the area of thicker clouds with the misty, hazy envelope.

To watch clouds, and see clumping clouds of the cumulonimbus type to the south, and clear skies to the north, with a flow of clouds welling up from south to north, if you watch the northernmost clouds you will see them slowly disappear before they fill the whole sky. That is a pretty good sign that lower barometric pressure is taking place to the south, and if one journeyed south to where one finds the thickest accumulation with misty hazy cloud structure, that would be the place to start looking. Rows of cumulonimbus clouds are a fair indication that along the row is its cause.

The civilized thing to do would be to have just one agency in charge of the weather in an area, and prevent any other interference lest weather events go awry. Conducting experiments with different amounts of copper or lead in some particular area while other experiments of the same type are also ongoing, while not knowing what these other experiments are, doesn't help to establish accurate guidelines for the purpose of obtaining rainfall in the desired amounts. A country should assign the meteorologists any and all duties involved, and for the reasons pointed out, meteorologists should be the only agency involved. Disasters get prevented.

Since no experiments can be devised on a small scale to replicate what might happen in the real world, the real world is the only place experiments could logically be conducted. Unfortunately, in the real world there are people living in the area, buildings, livestock, planted crops, and wildlife. Scientists would be forced to use some restraint lest storms prove too severe. One couldn't place an excessive quantity of copper on high and stand there with a notepad recording the results while the whole area floods out.

To begin, all the meteorologists of a country need do is find where precipitation in the country could begin to increase some, and where it could reduce some. If no water shortages or flooding are taking place, and that could be possible in some countries, nothing needs doing. When conditions change, and some provinces start to run dry, or experience flooding, the experiments would begin.

This difficulty, that experiments of the type we have been discussing need to be conducted live, in the real world, is the second major impediment to further scientific investigation. I saw a University of Southern California Meteorology discussion on the television channel, and the speaker kept stressing to the audience that any ideas people were coming up with about meteorology shouldn't be acted on in the real world. Don't do anything, he said several times. It appears it is hard to coax them into the real world when there are computer simulations to try, and conferences to attend. Academia is where they plan to stay, and the dangers of this process described herein and the necessity of experiments running live in real time make this whole notion a very hot potato for all the meteorologists. No one is eager to take the first step, and be ostracized from the peer group to which they belong.

Lead atoms are quite unlike copper atoms. The submicroscopic arrangement of lead atoms has a very haphazard distribution, with no easy path for electrical current to follow. The friction met with by electrical current make it impossible for any current to pass through lead. Gas molecules and other atmospheric entities find no easy path to travel along in the vicinity of purified lead in a high location, so the barometric pressure near that quantity of lead would tend to be higher since the gas molecules are encountering each other more often, with no smooth path to follow.

Too much lead put in place in a high location would lead to drought. This should be considered an act of terrorism and be strongly discouraged by the authorities, after due deliberation and passage of laws. Barometric pressure readings should give one a starting point in the search for unwanted lead placed somewhere as well, but the search would be centered on the areas with higher barometric pressure rather than lower.

A large negatively charged electromagnet may make cloud development difficult. Finding an electromagnet responsible for undesirable weather might prove a little more difficult than a considerable accumulation of copper or lead somewhere high up. Nevertheless, when severe weather begins to erupt, or a drought begins, these possibilities should be investigated. Perhaps a strong electrical current could be detected from a certain range with some sensors. Barometers would be likely to narrow down the range of any such event in this instance also.

If you look up weather modification on the internet you will find that several companies already exist claiming to be able to assist with drought mitigation. The alleged techniques that these companies use varies. A lot of it seemed pretty unscientific. There is also a lot of mention of electromagnetic pulse generation on the internet these days. Some way of quickly finding such EMP broadcasts should they pose a threat to peaceful weather conditions should be explored. Of all the possibilities, EMP type broadcasts may prove the hardest to track down, but as it is also the most expensive and difficult to construct, other methods would find more use.

The United States and Russia each have a place where these EMP pulses are generated. HAARP in Alaska of the United States consists of 180 towers, or antennae, each 60 feet high, with connections, in a field several football fields in size. It would be difficult to hide something like that if some private citizen were to try to build one. The day has not come when something of the strength of the pulses emitted by HAARP could exist in a hand held device. Those that exist in the possession of governments now can fire at will just about anywhere and not be held accountable for any weather disasters that result.

Ideally, some further investigation into this kind of phenomena will be conducted by meteorologists. The chance that any experiments conducted could be sabotaged by other persons with an experiment involving some other placement of metal in some nearby location needs to be considered. If secrecy as to the time and location of a planned experiment must be maintained in order to assure the purity of the experiment, then the public won't know when such an experiment is conducted. Therefore, the public will have to trust the meteorologists involved in so far as duly recording whatever weather events take place.

For example, meteorologists plan an experiment with 500 pounds of copper. An opponent of this idea becoming public knowledge learns of this experiment, and places a ton of copper on an adjacent mountaintop, or building roof, as the case may be. Three days go by, and the resulting storms are now too severe. The results of the experiment are not released by the meteorologists.

Or, the meteorologists plan an experiment with 500 pounds of copper. An opponent of this idea becoming public knowledge learns of this proposed experiment, and places a ton of lead sheets across a nearby high location. Three days go by, and little or no rainfall occurs. The meteorologists decide then to report that the experiment failed.

It would be imperative that these experiments be conducted with as much secrecy as needed to reduce the likelihood of sabotage. Only then would the true cause and effect relationship reveal itself to interested observers. Whether those conducting the experiment are answerable to anyone and whether the results will be reported honestly and accurately during these experiments one can only hope. Results of these experiments wouldn't be learned by the public until a little bit after the experiment, which would be fine since the experiment was secretly conducted.

In the final analysis it may prove more difficult than one would expect to validate what has been asserted here by properly professional people in a properly professional setting. Obviously, if anyone over the years had happened to notice that this process in nature did what it did, they did not communicate this to the general public, or were prevented from saying anything by a militaristic government. Now, that same government could make investigation of this phenomenon difficult if HAARP is put to use ruining weather experiments.

It is now well known that certain guidelines are put forth by the military with regard to classified issues; what can be stated, and what things are not to be mentioned become realities that scientists dealing with sensitive issues face. If the process promoted in this book falls into the category of one of those things that the military warned all the meteorologists about, and it is taboo for any accredited meteorologist to mention anything about it, even so the military had to know the advantage it held for some time would end and the entire business eventually be widely known, due to the simplicity of the whole thing. Seems unfair to the meteorologists, studying a science, and then being unable to discuss it in depth, if that is true.

Many objections were raised by persons with whom I've spoken to the effect that if such a thing were true we would already know about it, and for that reason it can't be true. The possibility the truth is still to be learned with regard to this process still holds true, even if it seems to most such a thing would already be discovered. To assume HAARP will be effective one day as a device to modify the weather with, one would also have to assume that the waves that propagate from purified metals in a high location would also have some kind of effect.

The machinery creating electromagnetic pulses would broadcast waves in the electromagnetic spectrum also. Depending on the wavelength, high or low pressure could be created by these pulses. The HAARP experiments involve firing concentrated pulses at parts of the ionosphere, not just sending out random pulses at some wavelength, though it could do that as well.

What happens when HAARP fires concentrated electromagnetic pulses at parts of the ionosphere is that the area impacted heats up, and rises, and since the ionosphere is above the height of clouds to begin with, those areas below begin also to rise, to replace the atmospheric components above that have risen, so cloud tops become higher, there is a definite updraft, hail is probably inevitable, and so on. Watching what developing storms there are until one seems ideal for further enhancement, HAARP pulses could be sent above such storms, or slightly to the east, and the storm can become what is called a micro-burst. Hail, high winds, heavy rains, and possible tornadoes.

By contrast, a quantity of copper doesn't need the expenditure of millions of volts of electricity, and won't create dangerous storms if the quantity isn't excessive. Some specific quantity would yield a half inch to an inch of rain, it just needs to be determined how much copper would be needed. Not only that, passive placement of copper could also be a capture point for lightning bolts, a source of electricity for humanity, rather than an expense.

The impact that this discovery might have upon world markets won't be severe enough to disrupt agricultural futures. After all, the mere fact that humanity has discovered one more thing to help them survive happens all the time. Agriculture won't suddenly become the easiest thing to do on the Earth. There will still be work involved in growing things, caring for them as they grow, and bringing them to market after harvesting. Pests that threaten certain crops could proliferate in a wetter environment, making the growing of some plants even more difficult than previously. As mentioned earlier, not everyone will learn of this process, and those that do wouldn't be a significant portion of the population for some time. Things would likely go on much the same as before, but with some significant differences. No one will be trying to discover something that has already been discovered, famine would end, houses would remain intact longer, forest fires would get put out safely and efficiently, fewer ships would be lost at sea, people would be happier, etc. The overall impact economically would be quite good, but it wouldn't happen overnight. Land values would eventually rise due to the increased productivity of land owing to better weather, one of many of the economic ramifications of minimizing weather disasters and having a world economy using abundant water throughout that would take years to be noticed.

Businesses might exist after years that would have had no chance of starting without the stability of the weather. Had mankind not taken charge of the situation, resources that enabled these marginal ventures to succeed would have been entirely taken by the construction industry and the rebuilding of structures destroyed by weather, and they would not have existed at all.

New or expanding businesses could start with the realization water can be easily available in the area where they plan to do business. That already changes the business environment of many countries that have in the past been prone to water shortages. Businesses with plans in underdeveloped countries might have to do their own precipitation making, or explain to those in that country how it could be done. It would also change the prospects for semiarid regions in more well developed countries. Arizona already has some extensive irrigation systems built and ready. Add water, modernly.

The likelihood of anyone profiting monetarily from this idea is little, other than a rise in the standard of living that would be slow at first but gradually increase, as one thing leads to another. Certainly there are instances where abundant precipitation could produce profits, but it would be the things grown and sold, not precipitation itself, that produced profit. Though there are some expenses, it is the cheapest solution to a number of problems with the environment around the world. The arrangement of six foot tall copper coils tied together with straight bars of copper tubing described earlier isn't necessary if one has a flatbed truck with a lift feature like those a garbage truck or tow truck has. Lay the tubing along the bed of the truck in a row tied down securely with copper wire, and park it in a favorable spot. Elevate the bed of the truck to as near vertical as possible, facing west.

The problem with this discovery is that no one has any facts or experimental results that one can definitively point to and say, see, publication such and such, pages so and so, etc., where some persons conducted certain tests with exactly so many pounds of copper, and barometric pressure, rainfall, etc., was recorded. The truth still has not been determined. That meteorologists scoff at the idea as being long ago disproved doesn't convince me this isn't a kind of trickery, involving superior minds thinking that the lowly masses shouldn't be allowed to know these things.

I think that if a meteorologist read this book, he would concede that things probably do happen when copper is placed on high, but may disagree as to whether it will always do basically the same thing. Hiding behind chaos theory doesn't change the imminent usefulness of copper placements or its beautiful simplicity, and as scientists, with the final say in matters scientific, doing that fails the human race, and impedes progress.

If, once the truth is determined, no one sees fit to spend time or money on an idea whose fruition will not be monetary, but rather enhancements to all life on Earth long term that each individual and all wildlife will get in small increments that will go unnoticed, such as not worrying about the weather every time one steps outside, let the market do what it will. No need to force value judgments on anyone. I just hope the science of meteorology means the same thing to me as it does to the other 7 billion plus humans present on Earth.

The concept of humanity as an ongoing entity with no expiration date is pretty much the way things are. There is ample time to set matters straight with regards to whatever floats above our planet. Large scale changes wouldn't take place overnight. What is hoped is enough people share my curiosity and desire to see this notion described herein get a little more attention by the scientific community. Some time will elapse between the publishing of this book and the next step. That next step would be seeing a science presentation on public television about some of the weather possibilities raised here. The only way that can happen is if some group of scientists do investigate. Once that happens the human race will be on the way to a much brighter future.

Human beings are under the necessity of sharing the Earth with other humans as well as all living things present on the planet, generally speaking. We all know there are creatures most humans regard as vermin and would prefer not to share anything with. Assuming we all know that science deals with finding what things are, and how things work, when we find something that may prove harmful we record the fact and the lawmaking body steps in to oversee the use of such a discovery, and try to prevent harm.

If the ATF became WAFT, the Bureau of Weather, Alcohol, Firearms and Tobacco, that would simply be the way things are. Economical or not to modify

If we don't draft WAFT we are daft!

the weather, if we once and for all declare publicly that we are capable of it and it poses a possible danger, one may be sure that the government will enact legislation to protect the citizens.

Deliberations by the authorities should be step number two, after confirmation by reputable scientists confirmed the processes described herein are indeed real, and has danger in the assessment, since excessive quantities of copper or lead could cause serious problems. Sorting out who actually plans the weather and making sure that no one else interferes, with laws designed to ensure that results, would be the thing to do. Step three would be a short transition to where most people know that the weather is being planned to augment the growth of living things, end drought, put out forest fires, reduce carbon dioxide, cause extinction of hurricanes, increase polar ice caps, etc. It becomes ordinary quickly, once steps one and two occur.

It needn't be meteorologists taking steps to try to ensure that adequate precipitation occurs within any region of Earth, since that science has seemed intent upon keeping these details from the public, and fear the duty of making weather happen. Local city council meetings could easily decide who does what and when. If scientists aren't cooperating, it isn't necessary to involve them in such a simple process. Blame falls to those assigned these tasks if things don't turn out well, and most meteorologists likely regard chaos theory as being preeminent, meaning, we humans will never get a handle on the weather. Any attempts to do so would only make matters worse, and they themselves prefer not to be blamed, or even assigned the task.

Marconi stole Tesla's ideas regarding wireless

radio transmissions, so ruled the Supreme Court, before I was born. It happened that Marconi was one of Tesla's lab assistants during one of Tesla's more prosperous times and that is where Marconi got the ideas he claimed were his own. I learned that Marconi invented the wireless in school, decades after the Supreme Court decision. One more instance of how sluggish governments are when confronted with change. I hope there are new textbooks now with Tesla credited with the discovery of wireless communication. Could be that some bureaucratic decision was made to exclude any mention of Tesla in public schools. I never heard of Tesla until after high school.

Most of the countries known as Third World countries have the problem of not enough precipitation as a general rule, or too much, or both, at various times of the year. The weather problems they experience is a large part of the reason why these countries are Third World countries in the first place. Bangladesh, for one, would benefit once this knowledge is assimilated and, ultimately, put into Encyclopedia for the curious to learn. Simply the absence of tropical cyclones hitting that low lying country would in and of itself be a great boon to them, as well as their being able to lessen the impact of the yearly dry seasons.

Time and time again some anomalous piece of weather information stares us in the face and adds to a growing total caused by either global warming or man made metal deposits. A lot of these instances will never reveal their true cause. A fair proportion of them are probably man made, though. Wisconsin tornadoes in January 2008, for instance, almost certainly got a little help from some man made device. The same three counties in Wisconsin saw tornadoes again in October of 2010, and again in November of the same year. Southeast Wisconsin is not known for tornadoes even in spring or summer. I expect that someone I spoke to when I lived there back then attempted an experiment with copper, or spoke to someone else, who then did some experimenting. Investigation into what may have caused those storms isn't happening. If human hands and a quantity of copper were involved, no crime was committed, except the failure to request or report a weather modification experiment to the authorities in Wisconsin, if there are laws about it.

The stance concerning weather modification with quantities of copper in an elevated location is it doesn't do anything. Therefore, if someone had placed copper somewhere on high, that had nothing to do with subsequent weather events, and was just another coincidence. This one is a pretty strange coincidence, since the area, near Lake Michigan, almost never sees tornadoes in spring and summer, and now tornadoes have occurred there during the cold months on three occasions.

Nature is certainly capable of any weather events or they would not have happened, but it isn't very likely they would have taken place without an extra man made factor entering into the equation, like a huge row of copper tubing pulling Gulf of Mexico water molecules due north toward Wisconsin. The January tornado in 2008 showed temperatures of 67 degrees Fahrenheit, and there was a strong northerly flow of warm, moist Gulf of Mexico air.

Whether droughts in Africa in recent times could have been due to the presence of lead bullets in areas where fighting took place wouldn't be easy to prove, but that factor exists also. One of many possible factors. In early 2008, flooding had been occurring in Africa, still more signs of wet weather occurring abruptly.

In light of all that has been discussed, seeing any program about nature or the environment is quite a distracting thing considering that so many assumptions made involving environmental problems are negated by the possibility that we are fully capable of doing something about such problems. No full discussion has ever been made of these topics with the assumption beforehand that weather modification is possible. Even a simple nature program can offend the well read, as for example, a film about certain areas of Africa and the wet and dry seasons and animal migrations. "And then the rains came", runs the narrative, and at that point one finds oneself wondering what the intelligent beings who lived there were doing prior to the rain arriving.

A lot of the global warming documentaries are similarly flawed. A major theme running through most of these is that global warming will change weather drastically, wet areas becoming dry and vice versa, storms will be more severe, etc. That remains to be seen, since a means of changing things by humans exists and has for well over a hundred years. A recurring theme in discussions of global warming is that we will reach a point of no return one day where runaway global warming will take over and be unstoppable.

Records will in time show how many weather events destructive occur after this discovery is placed in the encyclopedia, and then one could compare that total with the totals that occurred before that for a comparable period of time. When a 98% reduction in destructive weather events happens, keeping humanity in the dark would appear foolish indeed. Establishing the results of experiments with copper in high locations, with varying amounts, in different places throughout the world would easily lead to stable weather patterns.

The only way to resolve such problems would be to create guidelines as to how often precipitation can occur for reasonable amounts of water to be available. It is not too difficult to perceive when an area begins to experience drought. Plants start to shrivel in the dry heat, rivers run dry, animals begin to die, and the need for precipitation is evident.

Planning ahead and assuring that such conditions do not occur would be reasonable action. When rainfall becomes excessive and flooding starts to occur is also not difficult to establish, so finding the happy middle ground where neither drought nor flooding occur shouldn't be too difficult. Nor would actions taken to achieve such goals be the subject of litigation by persons who are unhappy with rain totals, if as expected authorities assign these tasks to meteorologists, provided no bad weather occurs. One could view the meteorological community and perceive that those scientists are not playing ball with the general public, or with common sense, and a decision could be made to employ persons other than meteorologists to carry out custodial duties on the planet.

Any thorough experimenter would begin with a safe quantity, maybe four hundred pounds, see the cloud development and maybe light rain, pack up, and return some time later with more copper. After a few tries he would find the storm system to be the size he is aiming for, and assign the task to a crew on standby until needed.

In time the whole world will have standby crews with well established plans in the event of drought, or flooding. Before that can happen this theory would need discussion, and it remains to be seen if humanity can overcome the differences of opinion they all have in regard to this issue. One thing is certain; ignorance has not been bliss.

There are other implications of this discovery that go beyond the usefulness of the discovery itself. In the philosophical sense, this discovery would not further the goals of those who believe that a God created the universe. Once again, it would point to the sad and cruel fact that as humans we're quite on our own when it comes to dealing with things, including the weather, the occurrences of which are legally "Acts of God".

As the Boy Scout hopefuls pointed out so aptly who were excluded from joining for being atheists and then sued, we do not have His signature on anything. It has been noted that there has never been a President who did not side with the notion of a creator, though the first four presidents, part of the revolution, were an exception. Religious figures will not see this forwarding their agenda.

My problem with that is truth lost in the shuffle. In the true sense of the word, the idea of a creator is yet an unproven assertion. Besides, the whole notion of faith is flawed. The famous quote goes, "To Doubt Is To Think". We as a species are not faithful beings, at least not in the sense of ascertaining the truth or falsehood of something.

Humans are curious by nature, and discerning what is true or false is important.

We are the only creatures known that are capable of thinking. Discerning truth can only be done by thinking. The very definition of man is "thinking animal". To have faith in something that one has no proof of is contrary to our very nature, and a direct insult to a God, if there were such a being. Any member of the species who decides the truth is that unimportant abandons all others of the species when faith is chosen, instead of further thinking.

Leaving no stone unturned in the search for God turns up the most enormous universe, an unknown number of times bigger than our known universe, looking and acting like a wilderness in all respects, if we assume that what is beyond here is more of the same as we have here, with some really big black holes scattered around between any number of systems of galaxies. No conscious activity transpires to induce black holes to collide, nor are the beginnings of life the result of conscious effort, but a combination of various compounds made of lighter elements, very small, energy in abundance. The laws of nature operate only; no other directing force is present, or needed. Certainly life is a purposeful series of activities designed to preserve existence, but it arises originally not out of conscious effort by some agency, but by increasing complexity among lighter elements.

Once the status of a living discrete unity has been reached, one could say then that it has purposes and desires, unlike a rock or pile of sand. At some point the accumulation of things begins to act on its own behalf, rather than sit inertly. A polymer that reproduces itself in the oceans arose out of a chance union between certain compounds of the lighter elements; other elements combine to make phospholipid molecules, no conscious designer, and several amino acids come along in the same way, and depending on how these first pre-life molecules assembled, a unity arises with goal directed activity of its own. Nor is there conscious or goal directed behavior in the hydrogen pairs that herein hypothetically reproduce, or in any of the heavier elements that eventually come about. It all happens due to the laws of chemistry and physics, with the only mystery being how the first hydrogen atoms developed, and how long ago.

The universe has no eyes, other than those that develop among living things; no eyes on any large scale that would be necessary to consciously plan anything. Happenstance coupled with the laws of nature is all that the universe consists of. To see what is unfolding as the work of some intelligence misses the truth by a considerable margin. That life develops at all seems to some the proof of a divine intelligence, but we know how small the individual components of atoms are, and combined with the 2nd law of thermodynamics, combinations of some of the lighter elements are possible, chains of organic compounds hundreds of segments long, of incredible complexity.

The largest single unity that could possibly come about in the universe is a very large black hole. It possesses no power to do anything but obey the laws of nature. It will eventually collide with another black hole at high speed, and the ejecta from the explosion will in time become billions of galaxies. In a sense those black holes were the creator of all the known universe, but it all took place without any effort by some intelligence. The black holes just carried huge amounts of mass and energy with them to the collision.

No sign of God in a known universe that contains around 100 billion galaxies. Our Milky Way has somewhere between 100 billion and 400 billion stars. Considering that it would take quite a bit to create 100 billion galaxies and still more to create unknown multiples of that, God would grasp our rules of evidence, these rules of evidence having been invented by our minds, which, if he exists, he created. Knowing that we are curious, able to doubt, and have limitations, he would certainly have signed a document for us, maybe even have explained where he has been.

Not much likelihood of a visit, or of someone proving God's existence. There is a slight chance the faithful are offending the supreme being, and an even more extreme likelihood they are wasting their time. Certainly anyone who decides to believe in some God is free to do so. All mysticism over the centuries which never bore fruit can be abandoned, though, provided there is freedom of choice and access to pertinent information. Religion isn't going to disappear overnight because of some arguments raised here, but it could become very unpopular in the not too distant future, if the encyclopedia include our new ability as weather modifiers, and people begin to reflect upon that, after several decades of more living things, fewer disasters, etc.

There is one aspect of religion, how it began, when it all began that everyone I am sure is aware of, and another that seems to have been missed. We know religion began long ago, when only a handful of people were literate; the printing press came along in 1450 AD. Prior to the printing press books were reproduced by hand, one at a time, and in 3300 BC there were fewer literate people then than in 1420 AD. What survives must be tempered by the knowledge of the present day.

The other thing, which most people aren't aware of, is a rare cosmological event. A supernova of a common type, after the initial explosion, later will have a debris field surrounding a white dwarf that has powerful rays shooting from opposite ends. These rays increase in energy as they pass through the shock waves of the debris field. Though a very rare event, the Earth could cross paths with such a cosmic beam. The Earth could be completely destroyed by a direct hit from one of those if it came from near enough away. The cosmic beam would be so strong as to melt through the crust to the molten interior, and tear a huge gash in the Earth, out of which would spew enough molten material to cover the Earth, and kill every living thing, even cause the planet to explode. One from farther away would impact Earth quite differently.

Written in the old testament is the parting of the Red Sea by the hand of God, and the Noah's Ark fable, where it rained forty days and forty nights. A supernova remnant cosmic beam from far enough away would have spread out over the light years it had traveled until when it came into contact with Earth, it could have been a mile or two wide. It would have been a bright white light, very hot, as wide as two miles, moving across the surface for five minutes or more, like a solar eclipse. It would have melted some rocks near the surface, besides incinerating plants and animals as it moved over land, while over water creating vast amounts of steam, some of it the Red Sea.

Those two events could have happened, cosmic beam followed closely by flood. Since all the steam that was created rose into the atmosphere, it would all eventually come back down, and take weeks to do it. The forest fires created by the cosmic beam on land get put out by the rain that followed, and all evidence of the path of this cosmic beam would be gone in a decade, except for the predicted once melted rocks near the surface. There would be certain isotopes of certain elements that would be in greater abundances in a rock that had been melted by a cosmic beam such as this.

If some of those isotopes are found a few hundred yards from the oldest great pyramid amid a once melted rock, and still more right near the shore of the Red Sea, that evidence found would confirm the

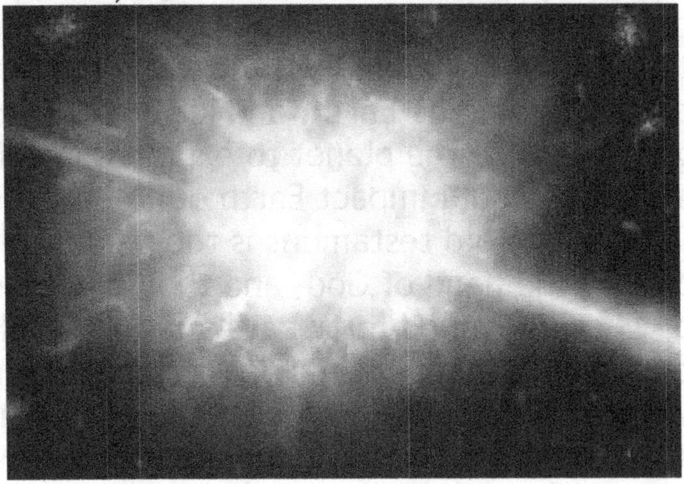

We cross paths with such a thing every 5 billion years or so.

ancient story was based on a true event. Since no one appears to have ever considered this possibility before, the likelihood that a search for once melted rocks and such isotopes has been conducted is unlikely. The oldest pyramid is from around 3300B.C., around 5300 years ago.

Going further after finding such isotopes the scientists would carbon date the once melted rocks with the unique isotopes, and my guess is they will prove to have been melted right around the same time, maybe a few decades before. The ancient humans wrote an account of the parting of the Red Sea, and of rain for forty days and nights, and it may have really happened. There were few literate people, no printing presses, far fewer words in the language, which all contribute to no reliable account from the frightened witnesses.

I see no other earth shattering event that would have inspired the building of the oldest and largest pyramid in Egypt, not far from the Red Sea. The thing I don't know is which of the events happens first in the old testament. Guessing the parting of the Red Sea occurred first, and the rain second, and with most of the other accounts just embellishments to emphasize what to the various clergy was a miracle could place the events a fable or two apart. Any witnesses that survived at the time would have averted their eyes since there was no doubt to them but that the bright light was the hand of God. Potential observers bowed down to the ground and covered their heads. Then, 4750 more years had to elapse before the development of the printing press, still longer until cameras.

Each book reproduction prior to then done by hand, one at a time. These new books were done almost entirely by the priesthood, rabbis, vicars, friars, monks, parsons, cardinals, etc., who were about the only literate people in the world back in

3300 B.C., which was also true in 1450 A.D. Surely others than the clergy were literate, and the number grew yearly, but the vast majority of humanity was still illiterate then. There are still countries where women attend no schools.

Each of those reproductions of books about the religious events gets a different interpretation and possibly a slight change in the manuscript as it is reproduced by the clergy person, and as the years pile up and language undergoes lots of changes, the slight changes and the poetic license taken by the person doing the reproducing begin to add up. The number of words in the language grew over years.

As terrifying a sight as such a phenomenon may have been, it appears that the only thing that could have possibly done this, part the Red Sea, was an event triggered by some distant explosion of a star, and the events that followed. This wasn't apparent to the people that built the first great pyramid near or on the site of this amazing event, the hand of God reaching down onto Earth. Unfortunate for man that as a species we had not developed astronomical knowledge to identify the event when it happened.

Were such an event to happen now, it would be correctly identified, probably predicted a decade in advance, yet still cause massive loss of life and flooding. I saw a show about the parting of the Red Sea that concluded the flow of water was stopped by an earthquake. A newer presentation came along about the possibility that a very strong hurricane with intense downdrafts could have cleared the water from the Red Sea. That to me was not the cause, not a miracle, and not what inspired the leaders of ancient Egypt to build a huge pyramid over. The account was of a hand reaching down to

Earth; for that to have been true, an earthquake or a cyclone wouldn't explain it. One can be sure it wasn't a hand like a human hand, it was the hand of God. That would signify a cosmic beam.

If some once melted rocks are ever found near the Red Sea or the pyramids to indicate the trail that a cosmic beam took that struck Earth, and we do have evidence something terrifying happened then, not an earthquake or cyclone, we can understand what drove early man to religious fanaticism. It still boggles the mind that primitive peoples living way back then would possess some insight into the nature of things superior to the current accumulated knowledge of all the natural sciences. Those people may have experienced an extremely rare and absolutely terrifying event, and made assumptions about the universe just as we do now, in a world with much less existing knowledge. They decided a supreme being was responsible for that event. That part of the world is still looked on as the holy land.

Surely humans gazed up at the enormity of the universe and pondered existence long before the singular event occurred by the Red Sea, and no doubt some were foolish enough to suppose some supreme being created it, thousands of years previous to that event. But it was that event and the notion of what occurred that cemented the idea into primitive minds.

An economics book titled "Human Action" by Ludwig Von Mises[8] has a part where the author discusses the notion of a supreme being, and the author points out that only discontented beings act. How could a being with infinite power want for anything or be discontent about something, and if that being were ever discontent over something that uneasiness felt could be forever removed in one fell swoop. Without limitations life no longer has meaning; a being without limitations would never act, or have acted once. Whether existence has always persisted or God created it in his only act of satisfying himself is unimportant, either way it is now a wilderness governed by the forces of nature only. If he does exist, he is definitely in heaven to stay. If he were to resolve his discontent more than once, then he would not be all powerful.

A creature without limitations is an absurd idea with no possibility of actually being true. That is why we don't find one in the known universe. We find stars and galaxies, black holes and dark matter and dark energy; also all the known elements. We find DNA and living tissue, numerous amino acids, phospholipids, but no supreme being. The worst part of a doctrine no one is to question is the idea of heaven and hell, which is pure fantasy, but to some of our species a big part of their lives. To suppose humans are just a larval stage of some being that develops upon the death of a human, and that this entity has two places to go is accepted without question by some. Reality tells us otherwise; a caterpillar emerges from an egg, and eventually weaves a cocoon. From the cocoon a moth emerges, that in a while lays more eggs. Nowhere in nature do we see animals who give birth to live young with yet another stage of development, besides continued reproduction. Still less do we find these two places where the hypothetically completed human dies and travels to exist except in the imaginations of less curious individuals, who accepted such assumptions without any questions, and have never pondered where in the universe those places would be.

Black holes are extremely hot and can remain black holes for countless centuries, and could be loosely likened to hell, and we all will eventually return to one, but we will all be long dead by then, and there is not a second option. There are no such places as heaven and hell in reality. The heaven-hell conundrum is purely a creation of religion, its only fruit but midweek holidays and blasphemy. Atheists are immune to the disease.

Ayn Rand's major argument against religion was that thinking involves a volitional choice to do so. We are all born thinking animals by definition, but some choose to think and others do not. Ayn Rand, as mentioned earlier, is a legally changed name, and could be phonetically pronounced "Aye 'n Rained, and I think that that is why she chose that name since any child seeing a book with her name on it might translate it that way. The choice one must make, to think upon the universe with an open mind, or obey doctrines long established based upon a faulty assumption and the even worse assumption of faith in the faulty assumption without any recourse to any rational examination is what gave rise to Objectivism, based on reality and reason, with no mysticism. She also pointed out that the church of ancient times has always stood in the path of scientific progress, from Galileo and before, and still does so now.

Ayn Rand philosophized about life, and concluded that logic and reason are the tools humans must use to survive. That Atlas Shrugged had parts where the author wrote "blank out" in the speech at the end of the book, were there because Ayn Rand would not include the word God anywhere in it.

Just as she couldn't bring herself to tell people how to make it rain, since she wouldn't have been believed anyway, instead she changed her name phonetically. Leakey, the anthropologist, was long aware of his Aquatic Ape Theory before he wrote a book about it, and expected disbelief, ostracism and criticism kept him from writing it for years.

To accept on faith that for which there is no proof is contrary to logic and reason. Assuming there is a God is "begging the question" in logical terms, assuming what one has yet to prove. If proof isn't there, a reasonable man would ask how it is you concluded thus. And no proof of a creature without limitations exists, indeed, not a bit of evidence has yet surfaced since the question was begged.

For instance, the first sentence of the Bible reads: "In the beginning, God created the Heavens and the Earth". As a youth I stopped reading then and there, since that was assuming more than has been proven, something evident to me even then. To read beyond such an objectionable first sentence would be to concede that the assumption made there had merit, which to me it certainly did not. Ludwig Von Mises pointed out that existence is ultimately given. We can do nothing but try to grasp existence as accurately as possible. Other realms that religions say exist are outside the scope of human senses. Choosing to think, not accepting suppositions that are unproven, is the only feasible method for man.

I don't see how anyone can ignore the laws of nature to the extent necessary to believe the accounts of what Jesus did. I am only referring to the loaves and fishes; he may have been a good fisherman, known when the fish were biting, or been adept at baking bread, but no reasonable man can be expected to believe that loaves and fishes multiplied miraculously. Events prior to the printing press by a considerable time as well. Fourteen centuries of language changes and embellishment by over eager monks, parsons, rabbis, priests, vicars, friars, etc.

There are other religions in the world other than Christianity, most of which I know nothing about. Taking the time to read the Koran, or whatever other religious book isn't very high on my list of priorities. I perceive that organized religion is but a deception, designed to control the lives of its subjects. There are countries where one is required by law to join the religion of the regime in power. Being a traitor to all of humanity by abandoning thinking is not a recipe for success. Those countries that are among the most strictly religious are also the poorest.

God isn't necessary for humans to treat each other with respect. The obvious benefits of free trade and peaceful cooperation between countries and individuals, the growth and development of culture and art by our society, movies, libraries, sporting events, restaurants, anyone can see that it is in their best interests to be a cooperative member of society. No need to beat morality to death. That a minority persists in defying common sense and committing crimes is undeniable. That minority should not be any detriment to learning the truth of matters of physical laws, or if such processes described do as is claimed here.

God isn't necessary to develop laws. Common sense will suffice, the reasonable man concept of law could serve as the basis for human activity without a deity involved. Right or wrong is easier to get to without the notion of some hypothetical supreme being. Right now, the entire human race seems intent upon tragedy, quite unable to cope with success. Success in this life is really not on the religious agenda. Tragedy has its place in literature and films, and should really end there. Life here on Earth may prove much more livable in a decade or two when fresh water is available to all land areas.

If enough persons favor it, religious and historical holidays could be abolished altogether, and instead, a three day weekend is assigned the last weekend of every month. The Post Office and government offices, banks, and many corporations honor the three day weekend. Gas stations and restaurants often stay open on holidays, nothing would change that much. No need to disrupt commerce with a Tuesday holiday. A bit of simplification in this regard has already begun to creep into current holidays, some of them are now being moved to Monday. Thanksgiving is not a thoughtfully planned holiday. Thursday is not a good day for a holiday.

When I worked in wholesale food delivery, the following Friday after Thanksgiving was one of the most difficult days of the entire year. Restaurants that order supplies daily had to wait a day. Other restaurants that order on Tuesdays, Thursdays, and Saturdays now needed to be supplied Friday, after the holiday. They were added to weekly Monday, Wednesday, Friday routes. As a driver supplying wholesale food to stores and restaurants, I have worked many fourteen hour days after Thanksgiving.

July 5th usually had the same effect. Christmas and New Year both falling on a Wednesday can lead to a lot of work on following Thursdays. Restaurants want fresh produce, and during times of holidays, more of some items. With regular routes produce suppliers have, occasional Mondays or Fridays off instead of the haphazard holiday schedule now in place would ease the work load at critical times. Courier jobs fall off dramatically the day before midweek holidays, no matter what holiday. There are sure to be other types of business where midweek holidays hurt, rather than help, the smooth flow of goods and services.

Traffic congestion during holidays only adds to the extra time necessary to supply restaurants that could not be supplied the day of the holiday, increasing the total time worked. Everyone doing the same thing during holidays intensifies supply problems to a considerable extent. Having holidays on Mondays and Fridays, and letting people do their own thing instead of declaring a patriotic holiday midweek would work out much better.

The simple confirmation of a cause and effect type relationship existing and it's placement in encyclopedia would be all that was ever needed for the entire human population to start taking advantage of an increase in precipitation from time to time. The things humanity has worked out end up in encyclopedia, and is there for those who seek it out. Once the knowledge involved in this presentation is present in encyclopedia, the likelihood of hurricanes developing at all begins almost immediately to decrease, and the same solution that usually suffices in the marketplace, supply and demand, will stabilize water supplies and lead to higher precipitation amounts over land, and less in the oceans, exactly what is needed. Economics writers have long argued that simple human interest in self-preservation will solve most of our economic problems, and it looks like that could carry over into meteorological events as well. The occasional abuse of this knowledge would be safeguarded against, once all who wish to learn this may.

Let's return to one of the first sentences of this book, the stance of the meteorological community concerning weather modification. In light of what has been discussed, it could be argued there are five or six distinct methods that we know of that can change the weather. There is electromagnetic pulse, such as HAARP, plumes of compounds sent airborne from a furnace, electromagnets to attract or repel water molecules depending upon polarity, strategically placed nearly pure conductive or non-conductive metals of some size, and chem-trails from airplanes. We could have the Chinese for a sixth, with their attempts to stop rain by bombing clouds with water absorbing chemicals during the 2008 Olympics, though whether or not that was effective is unknown to me.

Five or six weather modifying methods conflicts considerably with the idea that only cloud seeding is known to help a little to generate precipitation. Which method works best and is most cost effective, the metal placements in high locations wins. Not only does copper in a high place do what is claimed in this book, it does it so well that the likelihood of precipitation within 50 miles of such a placement of copper is nearly 100% after 72 hours. 100 square miles is coated well, areas farther away less as distance increases from the copper. Further east of the copper in its place the storm could continue with a life of its own, and usually does. Places along the western coast of the United States have many places where the mountains rise right near the coast. Placing copper in one of those locations could see rain daily, with mountains breaking up the storm as it moves inland. Oddly, a storm front will grow miles to the west and move east.

Knowledge for the sake of knowing is an important part of living for a lot of people. A lot of non-professional people have a keen interest in science. They specialize in another area in our division of labor world. They expect the findings of the professionals occupied with the sciences to be reported to them. A shipment doesn't just not arrive from somewhere. Whatever has been discovered ought to eventually be revealed to them. After all, almost 115 years is a long time, from the first time copper meets atmosphere, at least that we are sure of, more than enough time for any patent to have expired long ago.

An examination of what might befall the world were this to be announced to the general public should consider just what the general public is capable of. A profound discovery such as this would generate a lot of interest. I doubt that means that so many people with pick-up trucks are going to try this for themselves. It means more people would buy barometers and watch the weather channel more often. That means any unusual change in barometric pressure that has not been planned will be quickly reported by hundreds of home bodies, people who for whatever reason spend a lot of time at home idle, or doing housework, and able to watch TV. Therefore, the governing body would be quickly apprised of any sudden changes in barometric pressure in an area. The acceptance of our

"She says her barometer fell"

mastery over the weather and the great weather that we all begin to experience will eventually sink in, and after a few years, the number of people watching the weather channel due to the novelty of that new discovery will begin to tail off, and could continue to tail off so dramatically that one day it could disappear completely, with regular news channels giving tentative weather plans.

The worldwide meteorological community would all see that worldwide participation would be most conducive to peaceful weather, since decentralizing moisture from the oceans by using numerous copper placements around the world would prevent huge storms from developing. Who will take care of the Polar Regions will be decided, and ordinary rain could get more frequent. If that is all that happens and everyone knows when it is going to happen, it becomes commonplace; some young people may opt to enter the meteorological field, most people will lose interest once singular weather events hardly ever happen.

As time goes on, and this type of weather modification activity increases, which may be happening already, it will become increasingly imperative that all areas of the globe be aware that they may experience a shortage of water, and are able to address that situation for themselves. In spring and summer of 2009 there was a drought in Northern China; a drought in Australia with severe brush fires; some provinces in India did not get a monsoon that year; the United States had two or three droughts and Brazil was also experiencing drought and this type of situation can only worsen, if ignorance reigns.

Not everyone is going to agree as to how much precipitation should be occurring in the area in which they live. The air and water are public things; access to natural bodies of water is usually made a part of law, no one can prevent other people from having access to a lake even if they own all the land surrounding the lake. Lakes, oceans, and rivers are not bought and sold; they are part of the public domain by law, just as sidewalks are. The air is also a shared resource among living things living on land.

Nor is the issue resolved as to how much rain should occur in a given area. People suffering from arthritis hate it when the barometric pressure falls, they experience a lot more pain then, all the joints in their bodies ache, they can barely open a screw on cap because of the pain in their wrists, walking can be torture for arthritic ankles during a period of lower barometric pressure. People ride motorcycles, and never seem to want any rain to put a damper on their enjoyment of motorcycle riding. Others use a motorcycle or scooter to commute to and from work, and a rainstorm is simply not acceptable to them.

Water is essential to all living things, and some rainfall must occur if life is to continue at all. It looks as though some people are just going to be inconvenienced from time to time to facilitate the continuance of living things on land. Having more advanced forecasts would help immensely. At least those the most inconvenienced will be able to be prepared for rain on schedule. Rain will happen, and knowing in advance when it will happen would be a considerable improvement.

The allocation of scarce resources changes all the time as circumstances change. Rebuilding structures that have been destroyed by weather does provide jobs. To improve the productivity of labor and increase the wealth of the citizens, retaining those structures that are already built and hence allowing allocation of resources to upcoming developments would accomplish more.

Construction would not cease if weather disasters were minimized. New construction constantly occurs on previously vacant land. Buildings are continually torn down on a selected basis, and replaced. With weather mostly beneficial, only those buildings that humans decide to demolish are gone. The path of destruction a tornado takes could have along it new and pricey homes and other expensive buildings.

A dollar figure would be hard to get at when one considers how many structures have been destroyed by weather or forest fires over the past century, and the labor and materials needed for rebuilding those have been withdrawn from other areas. A long time with little severe weather anywhere on the globe, along with forest fires contained and put out safely and efficiently could usher in an age of prosperity never before seen, along with bumper crops year after year. The earthquakes in Haiti, Chile, New Zealand and Japan recently are disasters little can be done to prevent. Preventing those disasters that might be prevented could bring some relief from the overwhelming tide of natural disasters.

A look at the Sahara Desert and the Amazon Rain Forest reveal differences in metallic abundances between the two areas. The Amazon sits just east of the Andes Mountains, where 70% of the world's copper ore can be found. Copper ore is only around one percent copper, in contrast to copper tubing, which is more than 99% copper. A number of pieces of evidence point to the Sahara Desert having more than the usual amounts of lead at or near the surface of the land.

The Egyptians used cosmetic face makeup centuries ago, mostly consisting of lead based paints. Mummies that have been unearthed and examined have been found to possess high concentrations of lead in the bones. It has been speculated that a number of these people died of lead poisoning, or at least had their lives cut short by excessive lead building up in their bodies.

Drinking from earthenware vessels made of clay that contained large amounts of lead is thought to be the cause of the accumulations in the bones of the mummies, since the lead would leach out of the clay into the liquids being drank, and hence into the bodies of the persons drinking the liquids. The reason lead is so abundant there is because that land area has some of the Earth's oldest crust, that solidified originally 4.5 billion years ago, and has never been torn asunder by volcanoes. It has been covered over by lighter elements, sand.

Between the Amazon and Sahara we find the

Sargasso Sea, the place where ancient mariners were becalmed for weeks on end. Since wind is what the vessels they were sailing on depended, this was a difficult part of the ocean for ancient mariners to traverse. Based on the Sahara Desert resting on ancient crust with a lot of lead, and the Andes being the largest volcanic mountain range with the most copper anywhere, surely that would cause lower barometric pressure on the west side of the Sargasso Sea, and higher barometric pressure on the east side of the Sargasso Sea. That's why the westerlies no longer prevail there. Winds no longer continue east due to the higher pressure in that direction, and also tend to back up toward the west slightly, where lower barometric pressure exists.

A meteorology professor replied to an e-mail I sent (this was my only response to over 100 e-mails to addresses obtained from college meteorology departments) that I obviously knew next to nothing about the science of meteorology in general or the weather patterns of the Southern Atlantic in particular, and that everyone knew the notion I was promoting was a crock. The world's largest rain forest is next to a huge amount of copper and the largest Desert in the world on top of an unusually large amount of lead. There is no other ocean on the planet with doldrums as intense as the southern Atlantic. My guess is the meteorology professor felt the height of the Andes and prevailing ocean and wind currents were more to blame.

The laws of physics dictates what occurs, if the evidence supports it, it must be true. That is the difficulty with weather phenomenon at present, since this discovery could be easily overlooked and attributed to mere coincidence, starting with Tesla and his experiments in 1899. There have been too many "coincidences" already to reject the idea that the weather could be controlled with a little time, patience and perseverance, in addition to having the truth of the matter on record.

The ivory tower stance common within the scientific community seems to be operative here; the chance of abuse of this process by anyone justifies keeping 7 billion people in ignorance. Dangerous or not, the truth should be known.

The means to build an atomic bomb is not easy to find. Manuals describing how to do this are not available to the general public. The difference between building a thermonuclear bomb and just putting some copper or lead in a high location is quite striking; one is a complicated and difficult undertaking requiring some rather restricted and rare items, along with the means to assemble them properly, an assembly which is very long and complicated, and the other is remarkably simple. It is this simplicity and the surety that abuse could be avoided that indicate it would be wiser to permit this discovery to become available to the general public. The simplicity part is also a sure fire guarantee that others could make the same discovery just by noticing the differences in metallic abundances and climate existing between the Amazon and the Sahara Desert, even children.

A nuclear bomb can be used for destruction or the prevention of war. The awful effects of nuclear war has prevented all out wars from being fought. The discovery of a process to control the weather would have countless peaceful purposes. World population tops 7 billion, global warming becomes an ever growing problem and now the number of people trying to find a means to counter rising temperatures, melting ice caps and rising ocean levels among other environmental problems is now in the thousands, even a million or two. Guess we just tell these million or two people to stop trying to solve such problems since whatever solution they come up with won't be used anyway, since whatever it is, if it works, it will work in excess as well, and be unacceptable in the ivory tower.

Once I got a computer, I e-mailed meteorology students and professors when I found e-mail addresses on College and University Meteorology Department web sites. The east coast has a lot of universities. I wonder if that has anything to do with the rather cool, wet summer there in 2010, and increased precipitation over the past 10 years or so. Of the 103 nuclear plants in the U. S., about 60 or more are near the east coast. Makes the wet weather there even more unusual. No reply from any of the meteorologists but one to speak of.

Authorities are currently at a standstill since it has not been confirmed by scientists that human activity could change the weather as dramatically as I argue it can. Were what I have been asserting turned out to be the truth and that was successfully determined and placed in encyclopedia, then the authorities wheels would be free to spin based on the new information, confirmed by reputable scientists. Legislative bodies would draft laws such as summarized, one agency would do the weather and the public would not be permitted to meddle. If the new knowledge never makes the encyclopedia, misadventures with weather will most likely only get worse. Tragedy or success, and the past 114 years tragedy has filled the screen in the weather arena.

Chapter 6. The New Versus the Old

Been to the top of the mountain

JB

Desalinization plants have been built, are in the planning stages, or are being proposed in a number of locations around the world. The expense of building a desalinization plant for fresh water far exceeds the cost of timely placement of copper in a high location. Water in the form of precipitation will do all the irrigating, all that is needed is water channels here and there. Building a huge factory to produce steam from sea water, make it condense, and then collect the water, drip by drip, at a cost of billions of dollars when better water distribution is available at a cost of one ten millionth of the price of the desalinization plant doesn't make sense. The huge quantities of water available through rainfall and the wide distribution of water make it clear that using copper to create storms is the way to go. One robust storm provides more water than a desalinization plant could produce in a month, spread out all over a fair sized area. Desalinization plants also will do nothing to stop flooding, which is also possible with the processes of this discovery that have been elaborated.

Here we have an example of what happens when pertinent information is left out of encyclopedia of the world. In a possible scenario, a dry country builds a desalinization plant. The engineers hired to design the desalinization plant didn't have all the information herein available to them. The government agent who hired them didn't know it either, that is why they chose to build the plant.

If the engineers had known, they would have pointed out to the government agent that a better way of obtaining fresh water had been developed; either way, information needed to be stored and available, and it wasn't. Now every citizen of that country is paying the price for water purification, through taxes or inflation. Huge bad investments add up. Hopefully, no new desalinization plants will be the rule in the not too distant future.

The polar ice caps are melting at an increasing rate, and the only way to counter this potentially devastating inevitability while reducing fossil fuel emissions would be to load the poles with copper during the winter time at the respective poles and hence cause more snow to fall thereby rebuilding the ice caps. Now there are permanent settlements in both polar regions. Again, the encyclopedia could play a big role in what those people do in the polar regions. For one, a lot of time they are indoors and most of them read at least some of the time.

This looks to be the highest point

Most residents of polar settlements have some college education, after all, they are there to study the place. One doesn't drill for ice cores without some education. Finding out that the settlement they occupy could be in a position to help increase snow amounts on the ice cap from reading about it in an encyclopedia would have these prisoners of the ice volunteering to position copper somewhere around the camp they live in. Any break from the ordinary would be welcome. Digging out from snow storms is already routine.

The increased runoff from land would benefit the marine organisms on the planet. I saw a nature program once where the program pointed out the source of almost all the iron in the sea comes from precipitation runoff from land. Coastal areas are vital to all marine organisms. The larger creatures that cross entire oceans depend upon coastal prey for iron intake, which is probably as essential to marine creatures as land animals, or nearly so. Rivers like the Colorado that are completely used up by the time the water reaches the mouth of the river are not helping to improve fishing worldwide, or the health of the creatures living in the oceans.

The tiny trickle of water entering the Sea of Cortez at the mouth of the Colorado doesn't do much to enrich that coastal area with iron. Some whales rear young in the Gulf of California. My hope is that once this idea becomes accepted as fact and made proper use of, the trickle coming from the Colorado would eventually be a more robust runoff, and together with other means of generating electricity besides building dams could one day make possible the tearing down of some of the dams already built, returning some river systems to a natural state. As dams wear out, and repairing the dam versus adopting new technologies is weighed, one by one the dams will come down.

Plants and animals in the wild, some nearing extinction, would all begin to have an easier time with water more wisely distributed around Earth. When one looks at what mankind has done to feed the growing populations of people over the years since the Americas were found, it's the least we could do for creatures in the wild. The North American Bison nearly went extinct. The dodo bird and passenger pigeon are extinct as are a number of less well known creatures and plants. Over 100 amphibians went extinct over the past century.

The downward spiral of living things in the wild that has gone on since mankind began encroaching upon territory that was once occupied only by wild life could be reversed. It surely adds to one's enjoyment of nature if one really sees wild animals and plants in great profusion if one were to travel to a national park. Humans happening to be micro managing the weather to provide water for living things there isn't going to detract from the beauty of the wilderness. Such activity would help a great deal in assuring that wild things grow, and one's chances of seeing some rare creature or plant go up, in addition to more wild populations in general.

No trace of what is taking place with the weather would appear as an unwelcome change in the wild. Modifying the weather involves no building of fences or any other thing to impede the movement of animals in the wild. Something placed somewhere in the area periodically poses no danger to the living things near it. The animals walk around it.

If, for example, the southwestern U.S. embarked

upon a weather modification program designed to provide a decent sized storm about every ten days during spring and summer, and perhaps once a week in fall and winter, the numbers of desert rabbits and tortoises, various birds, and the plants in the area would begin to increase. In a decade it might be possible to hunt desert rabbits in the southwest. Mountain lions would see an increase in populations after a while with fast reproducing desert rabbits in greater abundance. Open season on mountain lions could become necessary.

After a while, driving through the area could be more interesting with more plants and animals around. Problems will inevitably arise when some wildlife encroach upon human settlements, but that happens routinely already. Moose walk into Alaskan towns often, and deer, bear and lions occasionally wander into towns all over the United States. Some of the countries where primates live have problems with thieving monkeys every day.

Incursions into human areas by wildlife could increase with greater populations of wild animals, but these incursions might decrease because the animals are able to find enough to eat in the wild. Bears don't visit human habitations for company. They are there searching for something to eat, perhaps because the food to be found in the wild is not a sustainable amount at the moment.

The question of what happens to wilderness areas and how weather modification will impact upon wild plants and animals will just have to wait until enough time has gone by to make a review. With the use of such devices as described herein, there is little doubt but that increased populations of living things in the wild will result.

Humans have always forced their way into wild areas and built settlements where wildlife wasn't far away and tended to encroach, so nothing is really going to change substantially. Land owners are faced with the decision to build a fence or wall, bring in cats to keep out mice, dogs to fend off wolves and mountain lions. A settlement seems more apt where there are lots of plants and animals, and fresh water, as opposed to a desert area.

Whether this increase in populations of animals in the wild causes further problems for humankind, that is quite possible. Perhaps we will see more locust plagues, further trouble with African honey bees, more problems with nesting birds, more outbreaks of mosquito borne illnesses, etc. None of the problems that wild populations could present would be problems humans have never seen before. But then, wild populations have never had weather conditions optimized for them before.

Perhaps some creatures become too numerous and pose such a problem that the only way to stop the problem creatures would be to stop any and all rainfall in a certain area until the creatures die off. Fortunately, the theory gives us a way to do that. Any rapid population explosion of some disease vector animal or whatever kind of problem plant or animal will start out locally, and if local health authorities are vigilant, could be stopped before spreading around the world.

Life is by necessity opportunistic. A Python now in Florida doesn't bemoan the loss of its ancestral home, it welcomes all the new types of food it can eat in the Everglades. So many species have moved to new areas recently because of human activity it will be next to impossible to eradicate the new residents. Before human beings having exotic pets, migrations have occurred in the natural world also. Plants and animals all will try to expand the range of the species. Whether a change of habitat happens naturally or via human carelessness, the universe isn't going to make a distinction. The entire Earth is a possible habitat for every living organism.

Some can only live on land, others in the sea, but each creature can establish itself in other locations, and circle the globe, by land or sea. Almost any bird or other flying creature has a step up on land animals and are capable of expanding its habitat. Land animals are confined to the land mass, for the most part, and a freshwater fish in a lake with no outlet is stuck until a flood happens.

Increasing precipitation in dry areas means changing conditions for cacti. Cacti do not find water inimical. They will develop a means of using the extra water. Cacti will evolve. We will be able to witness evolution. In time, new plant material will start to make an appearance on cacti, like leaves, and some of the water storage cells that are no longer useful will die off. A change would be triggered in the plant DNA by the rainfall.

The possibility that cacti could go extinct is real, except for those in controlled environments such as a greenhouse. They could be overrun by plant species that grow much faster to the extent they could be choked out of existence. Desert locations might want to proceed slowly and gradually with increased precipitation to allow local fauna to acclimatize itself to the change, and to slow down invasive species. There are some who argue that climate change should be allowed to proceed, and let survival of the fittest determine whether cacti, plants that developed in arid land areas with adaptations allowing them to survive extended drought, survive wetter climates.

The whole idea of interfering with nature will meet with opposition, though only benefits could be seen as a result. Even global warming fanatics will not accept this process even though it introduces an easy solution to that problem. Nature, however it comes, is for some mystical reason better than having perfect growing seasons, an absence of harmful weather, and higher polar ice caps.

Optimizing the weather would cause populations in the wild to double and triple but is no substitute for the real thing, that which happens if man does nothing. There is also crisis creation for the purpose of generating grant money for the environmental scientists who continually predict doomsday, yet another group without success on their agenda.

Barometric pressure is always higher on land than over sea, but we are exacerbating that condition with our civilization. One must realize that human activity modifies the weather in more subtle ways already, not the kind of planned storm making or stopping that is being discussed here but simply higher barometric pressure over land. Nature, what one refers to when the course of natural events culminates in rain, drought, flooding, is only the merest happenstance, and in this day and age, would lead to drought more often than not.

300 years ago, there was not a single airplane crossing the sky; nary a motor vehicle or for that matter an asphalt road. All the hundreds of planes, millions of roads and motor vehicles will bring air pressure up even more so over land than previously.

Other man made things, all the additional asphalt and concrete, lead based paints, common until not long ago, nuclear power plants on land, all with thick lead walls, will contribute to rising barometric pressure. Add all the telephone and electrical power lines crisscrossing the land, and add to that all the deforestation that has occurred in the last 300 years, reducing the number of trees in an area with leaves aspirating water, and air pressure over land can become so high that rain might never come by itself.

Doing nothing and letting "Mother Nature" take care of things isn't going to work. Human activity has already set the scales against precipitation occurring on land. We are to blame for the higher pressure over land, it makes sense to lower the barometric pressure, create clouds and rain, with another process developed by our civilization.

Reforestation adds trees to land areas plus the aspirating leaves of each tree. Once an area has new forest in place, the forest should be able to recycle water along with passing low pressure, and there is less need to intervene in that area.

Happenstance could still lead to drought, if every other place on Earth decides that the only way to get any precipitation nowadays is to make it happen; could be that is how things will be. The wise are wet, the ignorant dry. The problem that surfaces from that is that the whole Earth won't work as a smooth, well-oiled machine if there are parts burning with drought. The ignorant will have to join the 21st century.

Every major land area on Earth has records of average rainfall; taking precipitation amounts from years with bumper crops in each area provides experimenters with an optimum level to be reached. That level could be reached without any flooding, surely. Land areas increase precipitation by 60% while ocean rainfall decreases 40%, and it is unlikely that those changes would have repercussions; mother nature doesn't keep track. If some weather patterns begin to develop that are unlikely to develop into peaceful weather, plans can be in effect and changes can be wrought then, too.

The increased use of this device would be a great help in reducing air pollution. Cities with smog problems like Mexico City and Los Angeles could plan on more frequent rain to cleanse the air more often. Most of the carbon dioxide would end up in the oceans, but the air gets cleansed of it. People with asthma would have an easier time.

Precipitation is about the only effective way CO_2 and any other pollutants can be reduced, once the pollutants are airborne, except for increasing amounts of photosynthesis. A recent study suggests that rising carbon dioxide levels in the air, which are absorbed by the oceans may make the oceans too acidic and cause, perhaps, mass extinction of a considerable percentage of marine life. A lot of the coral reefs are struggling, and things could worsen.

The larger populations and sizes of plants that would come about from increased precipitation over land areas removes a greater amount of CO_2 through photosynthesis. Increased precipitation over land areas removes water from the oceans and fills rivers, lakes and aquifers. Even allowing desert dwellers to use water without fear of running out would help keep ocean levels below dangerous levels to some small extent. In Las Vegas, were I to wash my car in my driveway, I could be fined for water wasting.

750,000 residents washing cars amounts to a sizable amount of water detained on land.

There has been some research on funneling air into CO_2 scrubbers that remove the CO_2 that comes in and release air free of it, but whether that idea will be developed on a large scale remains to be seen. At least we are beginning to see some scientists looking at things that could be done on a large scale, encompassing planet wide activities.

We may see the day when teams of scientists or some environmental groups design and put to use several dozen large scale CO_2 scrubbers around the world, significantly reducing carbon dioxide. It would help if that was also accompanied by a more sensible approach to weather modification by meteorologists. Every additional rain storm, or even cloud over land slows global warming, postponing doomsday a little longer, until we are out of the mess without losing coastal cities.

Weather forecasting could be a planning event. Should a rain event be planned, there would be no reason not to tell the public about it; people could plan accordingly. Boating outings could be planned for the days between rain events. This could be a revolution in advanced planning.

After twenty years, organizations like pro baseball might begin to schedule games and days off in sync with the forecast, which by then would be 100% accurate. Fewer plans ruined by storms, from the smallest acts of people on a stroll, to sporting teams playing for a sports championship.

Forest fires have been fought in some events for weeks, with fatalities occurring among the fire fighters. The Forest Service continually monitors forested areas, and are aware of a forest fire an hour or two after one starts. Upon reviewing wind conditions and seeing a chance of the fire growing into one becoming difficult to contain, some copper could be air lifted by helicopter to a strategic place and begin its seventy-two hour storm incubation within three or four hours of a possibly serious fire. The fire fighters could concentrate on containment until the storm arrives, angled tilt to the copper.

Earlier, it was pointed out that winds of the prevailing westerlies could be reduced by creating a path of least resistance that countermanded the prevailing westerlies by an adjustable angle. When placing copper somewhere high up to create rainfall to put out a forest fire, those doing this should try to position the copper so as to minimize the wind in the area as well, and that could help reduce how far the fire spreads before precipitation arrives.

With use of the process by careful meteorologists few areas would be prone to forest fires because most places would be receiving enough rainfall to keep the vegetation moist, and unlikely to burn out of control, although in the case of arson or accident a fire would still be possible between planned rain events. A lot of mountainous areas won't remain moist due to the steep angle of descent of ground water, so forest fires in mountainous areas would still be a possibility.

Windmill farms could use horizontally placed copper to augment the wind and increase the yield of the windmills. Eventually certain areas will have designations assigned to them based on what economic activity is happening there. Places where windmill farms are in abundance will have a windy designation. Those places concentrating on growing litchi trees, or other wind sensitive plants would have a calm designation. Southern California has a big windmill farm, and a lot of agriculture at the same time, not far from the windmills. How that will work out will take time. Many plants can thrive in windy climates, root type edibles like potatoes, onions and carrots. After a long time the windmills might get moved out to sea.

Shipping could see an improvement worldwide. Few ships would be lost at sea if shipping lanes could be freed of storms. A ship laden with a ton or two of lead on its deck could patrol along the edge of often used shipping lanes and intervene between approaching storms, causing them to change direction or weaken in intensity, or both.

The ocean is basically flat, and air pressure is on average much lower out over the oceans than on land. On land areas the uneven terrain, the lower percentage of water molecules evaporating skyward, and the extreme temperature changes between night and day all contribute to rising barometric pressure. Now one can add human activities to factors raising air pressure over land.

Diverting the free floating molecules in our atmosphere toward land is possible, and together with the diversion of water vapor toward the poles would cripple huge storms, and make ocean travel safer in and of itself, even without a vessel carrying lead on patrol. After a time, with all the major land areas intent upon an ample supply of water, the oceans could wind up flat as glass and atmospherically dry as a bone for the most part. The only time precipitation would be found in the oceans is when some islands chose to have some. The oceans are huge, and even once all land areas are diverting water from the seas, there would still be some water vapor above the oceans in the air, hopefully an amount that favors human purposes.

Rising ocean levels is the prediction from global warming alarmists. All important information has not been gathered, or not enough to know with certainty what the future holds in this regard. There could possibly be nothing to fear; our puny efforts are overrun by the inexorable changes that the Earth goes through, and temperatures could start declining on their own.

The radio waves NASA detected in 2006 now means a realistic estimate of the future in this regard is global warming will continue, since we are now being flooded by a new source of hydrogen. Yet another big bang happening somewhere around the known universe would do that. New hydrogen in increased amounts means greater output by the sun, more water, and melting ice caps.

Global warming is a good thing for people who live in cold climates, and if it eventually happens the end result before some ice age would probably be good. If the Earth is on a warming trend, with or without humans burning fossil fuels, there is little we will be able to do about it but reap the benefits of longer growing seasons and more arable land. Efforts to maximize polar ice caps and add more water to the land will slow the warming trend down some, maybe enough to make the transition easier.

For all we know, we have our hands on Earth's thermostat and just don't realize it. Years will have to elapse with this solution working to see if worldwide temperatures aren't more easily controlled. With worldwide use the cloud cover over land would be enormous. The greater plant growth that comes about from plentiful precipitation occurring worldwide ramps up photosynthesis to a much higher level, reducing CO_2. The polar ice caps could be huge after a decade of more snow.

We can throw in the cost of searching for dark matter and dark energy, when figuring the costs of letting this slip through our fingers, if hydrogen is still coming into existence in the universe, and that is where dark matter and dark energy are.

Knowing whether hydrogen reproduction is going on or not and to what extent would help a lot. The scenario I proposed, that the ejecta from the Big Bang couldn't possibly know how to combine into anything after they fly out into space from the explosion of the Big Bang, and some hydrogen isotopes drifted into the early universe from elsewhere, and that hydrogen atoms are made within already existing hydrogen atom pairs that serve as templates completely reverses the order of hydrogen production in the known universe.

The current theory is at all happened quickly and is finished now. That is sciences conclusion, though it certainly begs the question of how anyone could possibly know what took place after the plasma of the early universe cooled. Another assumption made which has yet to be proven.

Standard model physics now holds that the Higgs field, created by the Higgs boson, is the energy transference particle that imparts mass to vacuum energy. The Higgs boson is spread over space/time in theory similarly to electromagnetic and gravity fields. As vacuum energy travels through the Higgs field, it becomes more massive, eventually yielding protons and electrons. The Higgs boson may have recently been discovered, but the standard model also predicts an equal amount of anti-matter as matter, and no anti-matter galaxies are visible.

The standard model also assumes the known universe is the entire universe, which has been shown to be incorrect, or at the very least, highly unlikely given how greatly dark energy exceeds dark matter, the current expanding rate of the known universe, two new discoveries involving things possibly outside the known universe, etc. The Higgs boson may exist, or a particle that size under certain conditions, but what it does in the three to twenty minutes into the Big Bang, based on the assumption that space is a fabric of some kind, seems unlikely.

Big Bang nucleosynthesis, based on the standard model, states that from 3 minutes to 20 minutes into the Big Bang all the baryons were created, and as temperatures cooled, neutrons captured by hydrogen created deuterium, and deuterium pairs created helium 4, leaving hydrogen and helium mostly, and a very small amount of lithium, which helium becomes through thermonuclear fusion.

All the other elements are created in activities within stars, mostly supernovae. Three minutes into an explosion so colossal it would be hard to imagine, and things are already taking shape, and 17 minutes later the universe is done making massive particles. Temperatures begin immediately to cool, and after 20 minutes the Higgs boson is finished, leaving 90 to 92 percent of the entire known universe junk that will never become anything.

If the possibility I suggested is the true one, the current state of the known universe would be the time with the greatest number of templates to facilitate more hydrogen or neutron production, and tomorrow there will be still more, and so on.

Quite a difference between the idea that hydrogen production in the known universe ended long ago and the notion that it could possibly still be on the increase. Computers could come up with estimates adding one million hydrogen atoms to the cooled plasma of the early universe, and seeing how many reproductions are necessary in 13.6 billion years to leave us in the state we are in now, with 8 to 10% of the known universe known matter and the other 90 to 92% hydrogen precursors.

If hydrogen begets more hydrogen by a process involving hydrogen pairs serving as templates, once stars begin to ignite and burn through nuclear fusion, the process of hydrogen production slows to some extent because existing templates are being used as hydrogen fuses into helium, and supernova make more elements higher up the table of elements all which began as hydrogen but are now some heavier element. The early universe consisted of bigger stars that burned out fairly quickly, resulting in supernova

My computer came up with the same thing.

after just a few million years, and that process continued for some time. Now that stars have developed after numerous supernova containing heavier elements like our sun, some have lifetimes in the billions of years.

Again, one would have to include the possibility that the product of the two hydrogen atoms of the stable isotope of hydrogen may be a neutron, and the entire scenario of hydrogen reproductions occurring changes considerably, since neutrons can remain stable if they join the nucleus of an atom already existing. If a neutron does not join some other nucleus, it will separate into a proton, electron, and an electron antineutrino in fifteen minutes or less if they are still by themselves.

Either a neutron or a hydrogen atom coming from primordial specks gathering in the space between the two atoms of hydrogen results in some dark matter and dark energy in the known universe becoming detectable. The only way the progression could play out is one neutron or hydrogen atom at a time. The matter detectable as compared to dark components would change, too slowly to detect.

All the processes that result in heavier elements than hydrogen coming into existence would all take away possible templates for hydrogen production. The greater the diameter of the totality of things we know as the known universe, as billions of years pass, the more diffuse primordial specks would become. Hydrogen is the most abundant element now, and will hold on to a high percentage of known matter for a very long time. For as many stars as there are now yet hydrogen is most abundant and dark matter and dark energy are a huge part of all the known universe, our known universe is young.

Now that galaxies are widespread, stars have all now likely established a steady rate of hydrogen or neutron reproduction that is likely to continue for another 20 billion years or more. Some stars will explode, others will ignite for the first time, and the process of hydrogen growth will continue until there are no longer sufficient concentrations of primordial specks to continue the process. Black holes will gain a good percentage of primordial specks over the next 20 billion years, and hydrogen will have continued to reproduce itself.

Eventually the percentage of matter that is detectable could increase to as much as 40% of the entire matter and energy in the known universe. Black holes would also have more mass in 20 billion years, increasing the quantity of all detectable matter and energy in the known universe to 90% or more of the entire known universe. At that point, stars would begin to run out of fuel, and the known universe would begin to go dark.

How long that will take is hard to say, and further collisions between black holes nearby, if that was what the NASA Mystery Boom was, could extend the life of the known universe. Star formation and then supernova could last much longer than just another 20 billion years, maybe 100 billion years or more.

The costs of taking nature as it comes will rise, there will also be the stunted intellectual growth of children to consider. Concealing pertinent truths from children isn't wise. The more we are free to learn, the more we can prosper thereby. Worse truths we live with every day, like guns. The sooner and younger one learns something the better able to adapt to the new information one is. Look at the skills of the young using a computer in this day and age compared to the skills of the old in that regard. There are still people alive from a time when no computers existed. Prior to 1970, there were computers, but not in the home yet. Quite a lot of old dogs learning new tricks. When children grow up in a world where this discovery is properly dealt with, and is in any encyclopedia, the brighter ones will never miss a step learning the new information.

Just because the last four generations haven't pieced all these new factors together about dark matter and dark energy and tied that together with weather events, and added that to existing knowledge of the polar nature of the water molecule, doesn't mean it will never happen. Better the young get as much as elders can provide to equip them with know how to deal with things.

Besides the worsening weather forecasts for upcoming decades, there is still the truth, and if it isn't addressed soon, anyone who cares to try a strategic placement of copper or lead of their own won't be held accountable for anything in the event that they are seen doing this.

They would be forced off public land. That would likely be all the repercussions. If such a strategic placement were to occur on private property and no one investigates any changes in air pressure, the deed could be done without being seen.

Mischief such as described might not always be mischief, if no one else seems to be trying to do this, and there is a drought ongoing, a lot of people might decide to try it on the same weekend. People shop in droves, and could weather modify in droves as well. That kind of thing left unchecked could prove disastrous if too many people got involved. Therefore, I think the grim truth must soon be faced for the world to see better times rather than worse. The only way it can succeed is by more and more people learning of it.

Eventually it will break above ground and grow into a beautiful breakthrough, and take its place amongst other great discoveries. It will become an accepted part of the routine of living. Nearly everyone will be on the lookout for unplanned changes in barometric pressure. The absence of severe storms and an easy way to distribute water to every land mass on the planet would make it possible to prosper as never before. Tesla will finally be seen as the progenitor of this discovery, even if the persons responsible for causing the wet weather of the first three decades of the 20th century in the great plains of the United States, and the Dust Bowl that followed is never established.

Chapter 7. Looking Ahead

Still work to do. Nature can be persuaded to assist
JB

I think any country that begins to modify the weather using the processes we have browsed through should conduct sweeps in a helicopter with a barometer in any area of that country that has seen a lot or very little rainfall in the past decade or so for man made metal deposits. Copper or lead may have been placed in remote locations and abandoned, and these lead or copper caches would need to be found and removed. Indeed, the desert southwest of the United States has remained unusually dry for quite a while.

The desert southwest is the favorite retirement locale of a number of people. It would not surprise me to find that the desert southwest may just be one place where lead has been placed and left there by some arthritic old codger, who is probably long dead now. This person may have been someone who noticed what has been mentioned, but decided to do something different, like move to the desert southwest and make sure it stays dry.

For instance, the heaviest rainfall total recorded in the U.S. in a 24 hour period happened in Holt, Missouri back in 1947. I happened to drive by there a few years ago, and saw a railroad track running through the area. Suppose a huge shipment of copper on open flatbed rail cars just happened to be sitting on a sidetrack there for a few days, and then the intense deluge that happened came along. It could easily be that someone noticed some event like that. I realize this is only speculation, but if such a process in nature really exists there is no preventing someone from making the causal connection when they witness copper in large quantities and a storm that followed three days after, or to extrapolate what would be likely to happen if lead in quantities were used instead.

The old codger retires to Arizona in 1975, finds a location high up not far away, and places 600 pounds of thin lead sheets from north to south in the location he chose, to block the westerlies and raise air pressure. He dies in 1982, and the lead is still there.

I'm sure that once the responsibility sinks in around the meteorological community, the proper steps will be taken ensuring that rainfall totals of the storms created almost always fall within the one-half to one inch range, and that is all that happens, with the exception of some thunder and lightning. It is hard to tell how often intervention would be necessary; once a chronic shortage begins to occur it would certainly behoove the peoples of that area, or the meteorologists entrusted with that responsibility to ensure that crops do not shrivel and wilt, livestock die, wells dry up, etc.

If such shortages do not occur, so be it. Action such as making storms wouldn't be necessary. Firemen sit around doing nothing because there are no fires to put out, as often as not. They are a safety blanket, there in the event of an emergency. The time has come to be prepared for weather emergencies in a similar way. It would not be an emergency with people on immediate standby, suited up ready to go like firefighters, but rather a group of people ready to suspend what they are ordinarily doing for three or four days, place copper tubing or lead sheets in a high location, wait to see the results, and eventually dismantle the copper, or lead, as the case may be, and resume their usual lives. Some semi-retired people could do this. In the event of a forest fire, where the heat from the fire and all the dust and smoke interfere with cloud development, it may be necessary to use more copper than usual to produce some rain.

The extraordinary minuteness of the as much as 96% of the universe that is dark matter and dark energy, and the abundance of these likely charged particles means that they are much easier to influence than stable isotopes of nitrogen and oxygen and the other 1% of the known atmosphere and this raises the possibility that soothing music sufficiently loud in a high place might be a feasible method of modifying the weather also, with the sound waves creating a path of least resistance.

Then one couldn't exclude the rain dances of American Indian tribes, or the possibility that human brain waves could be enough to begin a cascade of particles that brings about lower barometric pressure. If all we need do is think the weather we want, and it happens, it would sure be easier than moving heavy metals to high places.

Maybe placing copper somewhere just once on high for three days and informing the public so that local people witness the placement, have a huge party on the hillside, and remember the rain that followed and everyone has vivid memories of the copper sitting on that particular hillside, the memory of enough people recalling it once a week could alleviate any water shortages over the region for a decade. A video of the event could be replayed in a public outdoor theater once a week.

With groups of people, hiking expeditions could prove fun if each hiker wore a three pound copper bracelet on each arm. The upward terrain of the hike wouldn't need to be arduous, just a slope that yields onto the west side of some mountain.

There the group could picnic, even camp out for 72 hours or more, all the bracelets hung in trees around the campsite. An escape plan would need to be worked out. If the campsite is cut off from the path down by a swollen river from heavy rain, and there is no way down the hill, bury the copper.

A well provisioned safari may include a quantity of copper for rain making during the safari. Places like the Australian outback and the Gobi desert could be traversed more easily with a supply of fresh water. Ponds of water plentiful with rain happening make the trip livable. Wildlife would accumulate near water, so hunting could improve.

Once the paradigm shift is made, there is no going back. The encyclopedia must convey what has been discovered in the field of meteorology. Once that happens, people will see meteorology in a whole new light. The economy of the world will grow in a stable world where the flow of commerce is helped many ways by this discovery.

For example, a village in a poor nation sees plentiful rain for a few years. A family decides to open a restaurant in the village, something that has never been done there before because of the dry seasons. No water, no way to wash dishes in a restaurant. It makes possible many things, the water to fill the radiator in a car or truck crucial for trade. One could go on with more examples, especially where the existence of a chance to grow things would lead to many more new developments, and further possibilities.

Water is the universal solvent, besides being essential to living things. All the additional things that could be done industrially with a continual supply of water would fill up a long list. Making paper, smelting metals, cooling plastic parts after creation in injection molding machines, the list goes on and on. A country without a single plastic injection molding machine due to impoverishment and dry seasons could begin to see some of those, and, of course, all the thousands of things that can be made with plastic. Plastic pollution is a concern, but there are thousands of things that can be made of plastic besides shopping bags, things as hard as the outer casing of a swimming pool pump.

The number of well intentioned people will ever outnumber those with other intentions. When the entire world is watching just about every weather event the likelihood that all would go well and according to plan is high. Preparedness for disaster with this type of thing is currently non-existent.

Raising public awareness about what may really be taking place when disastrous weather strikes needs to begin, and facing facts head on rather than conveniently missing them would help. Since the whole idea of modifying the weather involves an incursion into public things, water and air, the public ought to be the first who are made aware of it, not the very last.

A number of things could go wrong if the Earth continues to heat up. Rising ocean levels would put many coastal cities underwater, and render them all uninhabitable. The cost of relocating billions of people should be added in with desalinization plants when one compares the cost effectiveness of using strategically placed metal deposits versus ignoring this process, and continuing as we have.

Land requires precipitation for life to gain a hold. No doubt the first land plants and animals left the sea and began to exist on land where precipitation was abundant. To have a process that could change vast areas into places where life thrives ought not be ignored on the basis of some obscure paragraph from over 30 years ago.

Places like the remote canyons in Utah could eventually be viewed as locations for human habitation. Cities built where nothing to speak of can grow makes the most sense. Tucson, Phoenix, Las Vegas, should be farmland or wildlife habitat for the most part, and eventually could be. The changes that could happen when water can be easily distributed could leave some of the southwestern cities unrecognizable in 50 years.

A little blasting, some roads, and modern cities can spring up in the most inhospitable places. Ecological solutions come easily when one can factor in flowing water and be reasonably sure the flow will not stop. Another Dust Bowl should never happen again. The canyons of Utah, with water and roads, and a little unique engineering could serve as dwelling places comfortably. Flat, valley land would be put to its most economical use, as farmland or wildlife habitat. Market forces would bring about such changes as this eventually, when water is abundant on a long term basis.

Wood could see revived usage, since new forest could be planned anywhere. My first thoughts about these things back in 1980 were about just that, easily rebuilt forests, and if begun by humanity in 1920, wood would have been put to more use, and still be going strong now. Trees are huge plants, and provide habitat for many living things; being able to grow quite a few more trees accomplishes many things. Covering Earth anew with forests as plentiful as existed hundreds of years ago should be the goal. Some of the rarer woods could be farmed more easily and be more available, at a lower cost.

Price figures on desalinization plants are around 40 or 50 billion dollars apiece. Add the occasional forest fire that gets out of hand, drought, flooding, hurricanes, and tornadoes, all stronger than ever, and we all might as well file bankruptcy.

The world economy cannot afford not to have this solution working. Knowledge properly positioned in the encyclopedia is all that would be necessary, human self interest would take care of everything else, including how to take care of misadventures with unwanted flooding.

Now that there are two possible things in the Cosmos that have been discovered that may well have originated somewhere outside the area of space that is our known universe, the entire Big Bang scenario will be reviewed and revised over time. The notion that the Big Bang began from a singularity, where all matter and energy, time and space also, were squeezed just prior to erupting in the Big Bang, is the first supposition to fall.

Hawking goes further than that, concluding that the singularity from which all space, time, matter, and energy emerged just came out of nowhere, and that prior to that event, nothing whatsoever existed. Years may pass before an official conclusion is reached as to the existence of things outside the known universe, but reaching that conclusion now and seeing where it leads brings us back to the inescapable conclusion that space couldn't be a fabric if all hadn't been within the singularity, since the singularity couldn't have happened with space, time, and other things outside of it.

Cosmologists will begin writing computer programs with possible cosmic scenarios where there are 100, or a 1000 times more systems of galaxies like ours, with x number of black holes scattered about, scads of space, and crunch the numbers until about 52% of the dark energy is contained in systems of galaxies and black holes at varying distances. At great distances gravity is so weak we would not know if there is more.

The idea that black holes are in all likelihood responsible for the Big Bang, and for providing the universe with new energy in general will get more exploration over the next few decades. Some cosmologists might even work out how long until the stars in the known universe burn out, and estimate how long after that before another Big Bang. I read an article in Scientific American in the 70's that tried to show how the universe would progress from now to the remote future. The author estimated how many years until stars go dark, and how long until quarks or protons fall apart, with nothing of growing black holes.

That quarks could eventually lose energy, and no longer stay together isn't argued, and I would be first to agree there are places in the universe, vast empty stretches, that have some atoms still in existence that existed long enough to have done that, but the vast majority of atoms, once stars burn out, are once again absorbed by a black hole. Even quarks that have escaped black holes long enough to fall apart will be captured by a black hole in due time.

We can all see these are events that take place over billions and billions of years. The known universe came about from a dozen or so neighboring systems of galaxies that blossomed, burned out, and were absorbed by black holes over the 500 billion years or more prior to the Big Bang. All the black holes, in 12 neighboring systems of galaxies, each around 100 billion galaxies, absorb the dying stars within and combine with each other, and collisions between black holes eventually occur, unique in each instance. Once in unknown years things in the universe enter, and eventually depart, a black hole.

It is never the same black hole. Nor do collisions that occur between black holes that result in an explosion need to occur an exact number of years after the previous, the universe will always have such events of various lengths of time. Some variation would exist in the age and size of black holes involved in explosions.

If it averages out to be every 700 billion years, or even in the trillions of years it wouldn't really matter. We have the long term itinerary for the entire universe, the exact time frame is very long. Most likely everything in the universe that is matter and energy has spent a far greater time within a black hole than being something thrown out from one. Black holes are home. They roam the universe for eons, growing continually. Now we are on a short vacation in the wilderness, in the cosmic sense, where 5 billion years is a trifle.

With the Primordial Speck Theory as the paradigm, all forces of nature are accounted for. We know where all the dark matter and dark energy are, and can roughly estimate their distribution throughout the known universe and beyond. We know why galaxies are so unevenly distributed throughout the known universe. What caused the Big Bang also falls neatly into the paradigm, a huge collision between two black holes, not the entire universe, which occurred in one quadrant of a much larger universe.

Nothing?! Preposterous! The whole universe can only be eternal.

It is also possible to extrapolate conclusions about the remaining universe which we have never seen, since the progression of matter and energy to and from black holes over hundreds of billions of years would always result in systems of galaxies coming about from collisions of black holes that have grown overly large, and these would eventually burn out and be absorbed by other black holes, a continuous cycle that never had a beginning. We have a hypothetical origin for hydrogen in the known universe, quite different from existing theories. To top it all off, we have an explanation for all the anecdotal evidence in the next chapter. What the primordial specks do to the atmosphere along with the water molecules gives the science of meteorology an entirely new set of dynamics.

The current paradigm, and the absence of confirmation by meteorologists of the weather modification processes that have been outlined here, was initiated in 1910 or so, long before the first printed article about dark matter and dark energy. Inertia has kept it in place until now. Long ago, far fewer truths about the universe were known, and many fewer inventions and devices were available. Nowadays that is hardly the case. We now have satellites, worldwide internet, helicopters, sensitive barometers, and a much more plausible explanation for how the universe comes to unfold such as it does.

Chapter 8. Anecdotal Evidence

It is patently clear to the most casual observer
JB

Alisa Rosenbaum changed her name to Ayn Rand, created an entire philosophy almost from scratch all by herself that was based on reality and reason, and wrote a number of books, both fiction and non-fiction. Her non-fiction works were philosophical. Her fiction books were also philosophical. I think it likely she was trying to point the way as a philosopher because she had some insight into the workings of things that other humans lacked. This discovery we have been examining suggests itself, though Ayn Rand never wrote anything about it. Her best known work was Atlas Shrugged.[9] In that fiction novel there is a discovery, and it does involve copper and the atmosphere.

For Ayn Rand to write a suitable mystery novel with philosophical overtones, poetic license took over, and the details of the discovery in the novel were left out. In the novel, rather than placing copper on high, and causing precipitation while at the same time capturing lightning and converting it into electrical current, the inventor had discovered a way to capture and convert the ambient static electricity in the atmosphere into electrical current. Lightning is the static electricity that accumulates in clouds, and is released due to the differences in the electrical potential between areas of the ground and the cloud with considerable static electricity within. To take the ambient static electricity in the atmosphere at its face value, most of that would be found in clouds, where it is released as lightning, so Ayn Rand is telling a story about a discovery as described here, but leaving the physics of the matter out of the book.

It is in the character portrayals that most of the philosophical overtones shone through. The inventor, John Galt, is mysteriously missing, and so is this purported discovery. When the heroine Dagny finally catches up with him and the two meet in his hideout in the mountains of Colorado where the invention provides the electricity for the small village there, there is even then no elaboration in the novel as to how the thing works. Atlas Shrugged is a kind of anecdotal evidence.

Further indications that Ayn Rand, in writing Atlas Shrugged, gave clues about this idea we have been looking at here, are as follows: Dagny tries to track down John Galt, finds he worked at the Twentieth Century Motor Company in Wisconsin, visits the now abandoned factory, finds some notes and some copper tubing. When Dagny follows another airplane into the mountains of Colorado, the other plane carrying the scientist she had hired to solve the problem of how to convert static electricity into electrical current, she loses the other plane in the clouds, and unable to see land, comes to a rough landing in the village where this invention is working.

Earlier in the novel she visits someone in New York, too late to stop the man from abandoning his current life and joining John Galt in the hideout in Colorado. John Galt had just left the person Dagny visited. At this time, hard rain was falling in New York. Galt's best friend Francisco was an enormously wealthy owner of Chilean copper mines.

There is a part where Francisco deliberately mismanaged the mines and the stock market crash it brought on was played out.

So there are clouds, rain, copper markets, and copper tubing in various parts comprising a web of intrigue in the book. There is even a nightmare HAARP scenario where the crumbling government develops a kind of electromagnetic pulse type weapon, and vaporizes a field of sheep.

Ayn Rand was born Alisa Rosenbaum, a Russian Jew. Her father had a chemist's shop that was seized by the state, deeply influencing the young woman's view of law and government. That government which governs least, governs best, would be one way of describing Ayn Rand's view of government. Her view was capitalism is the ideal form of government, but claimed there has never been a true capitalist society. America was a sad mixture of capitalism and socialism to her. She hated socialism. At 21 years old, she changed her name to Ayn Rand on a ship to America in 1925. Atlas Shrugged was published in 1957.

If what Tesla did and the idea we have been discussing were known by word of mouth in the early twentieth century among college students, maybe what the young Russian lady, a new college graduate, chose as her name makes sense. Right now I'm sure no old news article will surface from 1922 that has anything about this, so we don't know what people knew back then, whether people talked about what happened in Colorado Springs when Tesla was there. Ayn Rand mentions several times how the early twentieth century in America was a place where common sense was more prevalent than any other time in human history.

She really glorified that shining era, the Age of the Engineer, thought there was no other to compare. Her greatest work was Atlas Shrugged, and it took her over a decade, from an idea in her mind from long ago, perhaps.

In 1980, when I happened to first perceive the effects that I have been describing, a major drought was ongoing in the Southern U. S., and I wrote and mailed a letter to the Society of Separationists in Austin Texas, explaining what could be done to bring about a storm front. About a week later I saw news about heavy storms in Texas and adjoining areas with Austin being among the hardest hit.

These events just described happened. However, they are not proof that someone in Austin acted upon my suggestion and acquired a quantity of copper and sat it on a hillside facing the Gulf of Mexico, where the warm water generates copious quantities of water vapor. Looks like someone did act on my suggestion and placed far more copper than was necessary to bring an end to the drought.

Or, being close to the Gulf of Mexico is one place where only three or four hundred pounds of copper would be sufficient. The very thing humanity should by now be able to avoid appears to have occurred. This was the first letter I wrote to anyone about this possibility, and there was no reply of course. The possibility that flooding might happen hadn't occurred to me, and the news of it left me stunned.

The Society of Separationists is an organization devoted to the separation of Church and State, begun by Madelline Murray O'Hare, who fought some famous court trials concerning her children. Ms. O'Hare was an Atheist, and her children went to public schools where prayers were read on occasion.

She won the cases, and public school prayer in those school districts were banned. That was in the 60's. Madelline and two of her children disappeared and were assumed murdered around 1991, and around a half million dollars' worth of gold coins of the organization went missing.

I had decided to write to them in 1980 since it seemed they would not likely see any reason to keep this from the public, it does strengthen the position of atheism, and they issued a magazine. Texas seemed to see flooding on religious holidays in the '80s at a statistically high rate. It was not my hope that this knowledge remain a discovery known only to a few, or something used for less than ideal purposes. People waiting for rescue on rooftops along the Red River in Texas on Easter Sunday in whatever years I happened to notice was a setback to my optimism, yet it added to the likelihood of the idea being true.

I know this is all anecdotal evidence but these are all anomalous events, these coincidences. Science requires the investigation of any unusual phenomena, or science isn't doing its job. In 1982 I learned of the drought ongoing in Somalia and Ethiopia, and sent a letter to Saudi Arabian Bechtel Engineering, a division of Bechtel Engineering, a major U.S. defense contractor.

Naturally I never got the daily weather in Saudi Arabia or surrounding area, but in 2003 or 2004 an article appeared in New Scientist magazine online saying the Northern Sahara had been shrinking for the past twenty years, from Eritrea in the east to Mauritania in the west.

I would guess it would be possible for a huge engineering firm to try such an experiment, even leave it in place for twenty years. The drought in Somalia and Ethiopia continued a while longer, which are a little south of Saudi Arabia, not west of there were precipitation appears to have increased for twenty years, so my letter was a miss when it came to overcoming that drought.

About ten days or two weeks after I had written to Saudi Arabia, watching the Weather Channel, the weather in the Southern Atlantic was being shown where a hurricane was tracking almost due east across the Atlantic Ocean for the Atlas Mountains in Western Africa, something that rarely happens. Usually hurricanes track the other way, toward the Americas, in opposition to the prevailing westerlies.

That winter, 1982-1983, or the next winter, 1983-1984 I forget which, I learned of a drought ongoing in Australia, and wrote a letter to the American Embassy in Sydney with a brief memo of what they might be able to do in the circumstances they were in. Summer in Australia is during winter here in the U.S. Two weeks later saw a small article in a newspaper about a storm that hit Sydney, where it had rained "cats and dogs" for 24 hours straight. Once again it looked as though someone had tried what I suggested, used more copper than was necessary, or were so close to an ocean that the quantity of copper used was too much. The deed could be done with half the copper and no flooding would happen, but no previous experience was available, and or my estimates were doubted.

In the summer of 1988 a drought was ongoing in the Midwestern United States. Barges were running aground on the Mississippi river, soybeans and corn were shriveling in the heat. I wrote a letter to "Successful Farming" magazine with a remedy for drought, and a week or ten days later strong storms hit the Midwest with Des Moines, Iowa being among those hit hardest by flooding, that city being the location of the headquarters of that magazine.

Months went by after the letter to Successful Farming during which I went to the library to read the last edition of the magazine to see if anything was written concerning this idea that had been sent them and the recent weather there, and gave up.

I went through this experience one more time, in 1992. I moved to Las Vegas in August of 1991. On December 30, 1991, after seeing something on television about the southwest United States being in the grips of a seven year drought, I sent a letter to Rolling Stone magazine located on Wilshire Boulevard in Los Angeles, CA. Therein I briefly described how one could implement a quantity of copper in a high place. January 7 saw rain across a wide area of the southwest. I was relieved at the time when no flooding occurred to speak of, and began visiting the library to look through Rolling Stone magazine, expecting them to be progressive enough to handle the story. After several months I stopped looking.

Five letters where it looked like someone acted upon my suggestion none whom replied in any way. I also e-mailed my rain making idea to some people who were involved with trying to reduce smog in Mexico City and were using some kind of tall poles and electric current to induce the particulates to condense out, which was the subject of another article in New Scientist I chanced to look at when I saw the one about the changes in the Sahara, 2003 or 2004, and Mexico City has been rainy ever since, but I don't know if that is a major change for Mexico City or not, and no reply.

Plausible deniability is the operative phrase, it applies to everyone. All weather from 1900 on is suspect. Tornado alley may exist in the U.S. for no other reason than some farming family in western Nebraska knew about this process for decades. The current owner's great grandfather knew Tesla personally, their farm gave them a perspective on the storms in 1899. Under the radar for over a century, the family has been up to mischief with the weather every spring and summer. There were recorded tornadoes before Tesla was in Colorado Springs in 1899. We don't know the frequency of tornadoes from over a century ago. We know some happened. I suspect they are more frequent now.

The entire human fascination with tornadoes has gone too far. The end result is always some disaster or another, yet the danger, and the filming of these events is now a sport. As though civilization would rather see them happening.

There are many indications that something odd has happened now, if we count the exploits of Tesla and Hatfield, and throw all the strange weather in that has happened since 1900, all blamed on global warming, but possibly caused by curiosity killing the cat. The United States had a record number of hurricanes in 2005, including a good number that made landfall, and the following 2 years saw almost no hurricanes in the vicinity of the U.S.

Either Mother Nature changes her mind abruptly, or someone placed lead somewhere along the south east coast to ward off hurricanes in 2006 and 2007, something that wasn't done in 2005. There was a drought in the Southeastern United States in 2007 with water levels at low levels. It seems drought could be the outcome of lead being placed along the coast to prevent hurricanes from approaching.

I eventually conducted further experiments on my own, in the desert southwest. From May of 2002 until early 2008 there were half a dozen objects like circular bird cages about 6 feet high each and 2 feet in diameter, all made of nearly pure copper, sitting on a hill in the desert south west of the U.S. The first two years there were only five such copper tubing arrangements. The weight of this row of copper tubing was 300 to 350 pounds. The height of the hill upon which it was resting, on the southwestern side, is only 1500 feet or so above the valley stretching out to the south and west, so it had a small open space before mountains 6 or 8 miles away would block the signal from the copper.

The quantity of copper needed to be greater, and in a higher place, to see more precipitation. However, there were observable effects, mostly numerous small storms, thunderclouds dropping rain in small areas near the hill with the copper. Of the dozen times I have driven past the location, on the highway to Kingman, small clouds covering just a few hundred yards have sent rain on my windshield almost 75 % of the time. It was usual to be hit by several of these small storms either side of the placement. There was often a narrow band of clouds directly over this location, with the trail of clouds a few hundred yards or so wide stretching 3 or 4 miles in either direction from the hill where the copper rested, in line with the row.

When I first hauled the copper up the hillside to where they rested, I laid it all horizontally on a flat ledge and didn't return for two weeks, at which time the wind in the area was excessive. Returning two weekends later, carrying everything further up the hillside and placing them vertically happened next. Once the coils were tied with copper wire to straight bars of copper tubing, and standing vertically, cloud development became much more frequent in the area, and the winds settled down.

On Labor Day in 2004, I and two partners in mischief made the climb to the copper with more circular copper tubing and assembled the sixth bird cage type object. We took from the abundance of straight bars of copper tubing that were already attached to the original five devices. The three of us carried all six up the hill a bit further, and began our descent at 4P.M. that Monday afternoon. Rain began at 4P.M. that Thursday over a wide area including where I live, and since there is an hour time difference between where I live and where the copper was, the elapsed time was closer to 73 hours.

Once my writing was pretty well along I made a journey to the site where the half dozen copper devices were, with a friend, who also owns the property, with the intention of taking pictures to add to this book. After climbing around the whole hill, we found where the site had been, but found only a hack saw, and one of the copper wires that was used to tie one of the copper coils to a nearby rock to keep it from being blown over by the wind, with the loop that went around the rock still tied.

So the experiment came to an inglorious end when someone noticed the strange looking objects while hiking through the area, looked closer, decided that it was something valuable, and stole it. It must have come as a shock to whoever found those things, to see a half dozen odd looking contraptions in the midst of nothing but rocks, cacti, sagebrush, sand, and creosote bush. I have a few pictures included at the end of the book. Those pictures were taken by the land owner. He is not in any of the pictures. My friend with the sunglasses is, and yours truly. One picture shows when we first came upon the copper, and it shows that several of the objects had been blown over by the wind.

The picture looking downhill over my friend's shoulder shows the trailer my friend lives in, and several vehicles. It takes about an hour to walk down from there to his trailer, and a little longer going up. The theft we think took place in early to mid 2008. The last visit, when we did not find the copper, was in September of 2008. If one were to look at the weather in Kingman AZ from 2002 through 2007, it should show above average rainfall. The location was ten miles toward Las Vegas from Kingman. Come over Hoover Dam on the 93 southbound, hit the double lane 15 miles distant, and the weather was different then, to the other side of Kingman.

On a trip back from the Grand Canyon in 2005 along 40 west, we traveled parallel to a stream of clouds hundreds of miles long, thickening to the west, while at the same time we saw a similar stream of clouds on the western horizon, streaming from north to south. When we passed Kingman and journeyed beyond where the copper was resting on the hillside, we passed the point of the two meeting, and beyond that, there were no more streaming clouds. This all happened in the twilight to night part of the day, and when we passed the hillside on which the copper rested it was quite dark, but evident that the meeting place of the two streams of clouds was precisely in the area where the copper rested, after two plus years of resting there.

It is apparent now at the end of this chapter that there could be a great many other ways of placing copper somewhere that I haven't tried. Solid bars of copper, multiple placements of copper of various kinds over a few hundred square mile area, these are intriguing options to explore. Could very well be that a half dozen two or three hundred pound copper placements spread around an area would cause the right kind of cloud development to occur, and prevent tornadoes, hail and huge thunderstorms from occurring. Clouds might not clump into cumulonimbus clouds, but rather be more general cloudiness resulting in precipitation.

Man acts to further his existence, with limited means and imperfect knowledge. Imperfection is everywhere; nowhere will a quantity of copper do exactly what every local resident wants it to. Always some area will be left with inadequate precipitation or too much. After years to develop experience with what to expect under certain conditions, weather could see improvement. The very first years could be a little difficult, but practice would eventually perfect weather modification.

Chapter 9: From The Beginning

When one knows where one is going,
Maybe then one might anticipate what will unfold

JB

My interest in copper and the atmosphere began with a book, "Modern Physics and Antiphysics"[10], which I read back in the 70's. I became fascinated when the author mentioned The Absolute Frame of Reference, and the search for it. What we can distinguish about things and their movement in space always comes from a frame of reference that is relative to another observer, or relative to some stationary object. Though the object is moving, it is moving right along with the observer, and thus appears motionless.

Indeed, anyone anywhere can testify to the fact that, though we are moving at incredible velocity, we could be sitting at a restaurant enjoying dinner, and everything around us appears motionless. The other diners seem to be enjoying themselves, the wait staff has no difficulty moving from place to place, the famous picture on the wall seen sitting down at the table is still there three quarters of an hour later, with dessert and coffee. Nothing has moved, but that is only relative to an observer in a fixed location. Everything moved, but it all went the same direction. The passage of Earth through space goes undetected, the direction partly known astronomically, and the velocity quite considerable.

Our frame of reference is our own Solar System, since all within it is in orbit around the Sun, and following the Sun as it orbits the Milky Way. Knowing the absolute frame of reference would enable one to distinguish the difference between one square foot of space and its adjacent square foot of empty space. Areas of space are things that are not labeled in any way, are completely identical, and consist of mere emptiness.

There has been speculation about zero point energy that ties in with the absolute frame of reference and knowing one's exact speed and direction as well. The discussion began with Michelson and Morley, and the search for the "ether wind". That was the title of the chapter.

Michelson and Morley were searching for an ether wind, a stratum in space through which things pass, thought to exist to explain gravity, or the passage of light through vast areas of space, or Newton's Laws, or Einstein's discussions of how one observer, being in a different place from another observer, may see an event from a different frame of reference actually occurring differently from the other observer.

There were various hypotheses about the subject, of the void, and was anything in it. Also how, indeed, does one distinguish between one square foot of empty space and another, since we are sliding any which way between any astounding number of empty square feet, and thus far we have absolutely no way to distinguish one area of space from another. The Solar System, in orbit around the Milky Way, is moving somewhere around 500 thousand miles an hour. One could be to the moon and back in an hour at that speed. The problem defined, as time went on an idea came to me about how one might conduct an experiment to find the absolute frame of reference. The problem remains unsolved to this day, and many think it insoluble. Obviously I didn't solve it either.

First, if one were to try such an experiment the experiment would take place in a fixed location on the surface of the Earth at a specific time. Each day, wherever we are going makes a full circle from our perspective on the surface of the Earth. Though the Earth continues in one basic direction, at noon it is 180 degrees from whatever direction and speed it is going at midnight, to an observer in a fixed location on the Earth. For example, suppose at noon the direction of the Earth is straight up over our heads. At midnight straight down beneath our feet. This is the most rapid change. Every 4 minutes the Earth spins one degree.

Starting with the Big Bang, the things that become our Solar System are thrown out at high speed along with everything else. We may still retain some inertia from that event, so that is one motion, if we assume the collision of the two black holes that created our known universe, or whatever theory about it coming out of a singularity, was motionless at the time.

The Big Bang could have been sliding one direction or another while it happened. One of the black holes that collided could have been much larger than the other. The impetus of the larger black hole over the smaller is impossible to calculate. Thus, finding the absolute direction of things by pure mathematics might ultimately prove impossible, since one could never have the figure for other possible motions. After the Big Bang, there is movement within the cluster of galaxies that includes the Milky Way, our rotation as a star system with planets around our galaxy, rotation around the sun, and Earth on its axis.

Given 5 or more movements to calculate, and high speed velocities, the curving path would be as near a straight line as one could get for a short distance. That it is not an exactly straight line wouldn't reveal itself for some thousands of miles. That understood, one could find where exactly the matter in our solar system is going by accident. Lined up in the straight line all local matter is traveling in, there could be static electricity left in our wake that could be detected and collected.

This idea tied in with the discovery withheld from the world in the novel Atlas Shrugged. The most

Everything is heading that way right now

Intriguing thing to me about the book was the invention. It consisted of some device that captured ambient static electricity and converted it into electricity. The ambient static electricity would be left in our wake, was my conjecture, as we sped through the universe at incredible velocity, perhaps. It didn't occur to me then that static electricity and lightning are the same thing.

I even hypothesized at the time that since space is not distinguishable, in so far as telling which identical area of space is which, and the Big Bang being such a colossal explosion, perhaps the matter flying apart exceeded the speed of light, and could even be doing so now, since the universe seems to be expanding very quickly.

For all we know our limited viewpoint wouldn't tell us exactly how fast we are going any more than where or in what way. The thing to do to find the absolute frame of reference would be to engineer a kind of arrangement which would be easy to make with copper refrigerator tubing, aligned so as it flew through space, it was in a perfect line with our actual direction through space and be in position to capture static electricity. Possibly a funnel shape, wide at one end, and tapering to a point at the end where electricity collects.

I thought that would be the only way to really find the Absolute Frame of Reference, by coming upon it quite by accident after giving enough different tries to a length of copper, at different positions and angles. What was the rush, I might never find it, but even if I didn't I would still have the copper, and could continue with it, possibly refine the experiment with knowledge of the direction of the solar system through the galaxy at 12 noon in my neck of the woods, get a voltmeter, etc. At the time, a visit to Radio Shack or some other electronic supply store was next on my list of things to do.

Having determined it would take years, and

pretty sure that I would need to refine the whole experiment some to ever accomplish anything, but impulsive enough to try anyway, I acquired two continuous lengths of circular copper tubing that could be stretched out to a length of fifteen feet or so, each loop of coil a foot apart, and a foot and a half in diameter. I think the coils were three eighths inch diameter hollow tubing, 99.97% copper. My conjecture was ambient static electricity might accumulate in some circular tubing because copper conducts electricity so well, something that could be captured better along the length of the copper depending how it's positioned, so I stretched these out the length of an upstairs bedroom, and at the lower end was a car battery out of power, and the upper ends were by the one open window to the north, and the one open window to the west.

I think I noted the time to myself, and three days go by, and there is a storm moving in to the area. As always the weather held my interest. I went in the back yard, and was watching the lightning, and listening to the thunder. The storm was close, the thunder was getting louder, and heard in less time after the flash, and suddenly the loudest clap of thunder I have ever heard stood my hair on end and in that instant, translation of the name Ayn Rand by my mind into the phonetic pronunciation "Aye 'n Rained" like an Irish person talking happened, and then I perceived what had eluded me up to that point. My mind raced with the possibilities. That began my realization that weather modification was a possibility long known, and kept from the public.

Now it seems it was a dumb experiment that took just three days with no chance of succeeding unless some more sensitive measuring instruments were used but I did it, and that blast of thunder sent my thoughts instantly away from ambient static electricity and finding the absolute frame of reference to using copper tubing for rain making and collecting electricity from lightning.

There I was oblivious to the possibility that the copper tubing by those two open windows might have something to do with this storm that was bearing right down on us from the northwest, I had forgotten all about them, when that clap of thunder and the thunder bolt of realizations in my head happened all at the same instant. It was plain that the copper must have caused a path of least resistance which the atmospheric particles, being small, and having electrons, would follow.

Perhaps it may have had a short term impact on the storm in the area, maybe enough to bring one lightning bolt quite near, but it was certainly too small an amount to generate the storm, at least that is what I thought.

The actual beginning of all this began with an idea about something else entirely, then, and the first events where I experienced experiments with copper and the atmosphere were inconclusive. The epiphany, the thunderbolt, had me convinced I was on the right track. Something conductive, large, in a high place would generate a path of least resistance for all atmospheric components to more easily slide along. Later I learned of Tesla's exploits in Colorado Springs in 1899, and the decades of wet weather in the middle of the U. S. that followed.

At this point, I would also have to add that my brain provided me with a sudden insight during that thunderbolt; I tend to trust my inspirations if and when they happen. To have done otherwise would have been extremely foolish. Whatever electrical transmissions took place in my mind to cause me to be conscious of what I became conscious of was going on at a deeper level of consciousness where more information is cross referenced. The sum total of my being told me the truth, and I believed it. Lightning is static electricity, large amounts that gather in clouds and are released as lightning bolts. Suddenly the concept of static electricity being converted to electricity changed from small amounts collected continually to huge amounts sent from lightning bolts collected quickly.

I began to think of correlations in the real world that roughly corresponded to what I thought was taking place. A car while traveling on an icy road, for example. The car reaches a curve, the driver turns the wheel, but there is a patch of ice on the road. The car continues along the path of least resistance, there is not enough friction for the front tires to grip, turning the car, so the car goes off the road. Another one involved the copper reducing the amount of static electricity in the air, and that gives rise to the more conductive path, less electrical resistance. That area closest the copper, with little or no static electricity, creates a small vortex that snowballs and intensifies into a low pressure system.

Mostly what went through my mind was a rule of thumb in physics, basically why water doesn't run uphill. When energy is required for something to not follow a path of least resistance, in short, for water to run uphill, it won't do it. It will take the path requiring the least energy. One could conclude that any of the small atmospheric components wouldn't expend energy to avoid the path of least resistance, and are quite likely to gravitate towards the path of least resistance, that being the easiest path to follow, and also one that is being followed by numerous charged atmospheric components.

Relative humidity can be quite misleading. Water reaches the saturation point at 100% relative humidity, but the amount of water by weight in the atmosphere then seldom exceeds 3%. Water molecules are lighter by weight than nitrogen and oxygen pairs, so there would need to be more of them to make up the percentage of air by weight that they occupy. Still, if the actual humidity by weight of water in the atmosphere at the start of an experiment is 0.25%, and it must reach 3% for rain to begin to fall, there really isn't that far to go, when one considers that water molecules themselves will begin gathering along the path of least resistance. Water molecules heading to a location may be alone responsible for the observable effects, though falling barometric pressure would seem to involve a few other things.

To conduct a type of experiment to find the absolute frame of reference such as I had begun to try and quickly abandoned back in 1980, one would need a huge room like an aircraft hangar or a large pole barn, a stand to put super conducting material on that one could turn in any direction with control mechanisms, a 100 foot long super conducting composite material in a straight circular tube, sensing equipment all along the super conducting material, and a computer to monitor the whole event, while calculating Earth's position in the universe, motion of Earth's axis, orbit around the sun, and orbit of our solar system about the galaxy.

The Earth turns full circle every 24 hours, so 360 degrees divided by 24 hours gives us 15 degrees of arc each hour. If we are traveling along with the Milky Way somewhere around 1,339,000 miles per hour, that distance we travel in an hour divided by 15 gives one degree of curvature every 89,000 miles or so. Just from this guess, one mile would reveal 1/89000th of one degree of curvature and 100 feet is only one 52nd or so as long as a mile. That would be almost as straight a line as one could possibly get, without actually being straight, for the 100 foot length of the super conducting material.

Taking the 1,339,000 miles an hour or so we are traveling with the Milky Way, that computes to 372 miles per second. A very small fraction of a second elapses while the Earth and everything on it slide one hundred feet. There are 1,964,160 feet in one second of travel at this speed. So that is 19,641 one hundred foot lengths in one second. About one half of one ten thousandth of a second to travel 100 ft. in a straight line, slowly changing, one degree every four minutes, besides some other more gradual changes. Zooming along we are, and other curves in the path would be gradual in comparison to the 24 hour spin of the Earth on its axis. As we orbit the Sun, we slowly curve around it, but the entire journey is a year long to go a full 360 degrees and covers many miles, so the degree of curvature has to be pretty small. Considering that 30 degrees of curvature takes a month, we would be traveling at right angles in around 90 days in comparison to our current direction as we go around the Sun near one degree of curvature a day. One degree of curvature takes 4 minutes as Earth rotates on its axis.

To see how straight a line for 100 feet with one degree of curvature every four minutes, 4 minutes has 240 seconds, 240 seconds has 2,400,000 ten thousandths of a second. Half a ten thousandth of a second is one 4,800,000th of one degree of arc.

The orbit of the Solar System around the galaxy takes 240 million years to complete. The Milky Way is around 100,000 light years in diameter. To reach just one degree of curvature as we go around the galaxy would take over 600,000 years, so that rate of curvature in our direction through space would be so gradual as to be nearly undetectable.

Astronomers have gauged the Milky Way to be traversing intergalactic space at 600km per second, or around 372 miles per second, more than twice as fast as we travel around the Milky Way, as it orbits the local galaxy cluster. The Earth is moving more slowly around the Sun than the Sun is around the Milky Way, and the Sun is traveling more slowly around the galaxy than the galaxy round the local cluster of galaxies. The larger a thing or group of things is, the faster it would be going. The curving path of the orbits of things would also be a lot more gradual the larger a thing or collection of things is. We can't expect galaxies to turn sharp corners.

One would also need to know the extent to which the Milky Way is being pulled toward the attractive force in the Andrew Kashlinsky article. Some of the galaxies nearest this probable black hole are moving towards the thing at 3 million miles per hour, others farther away much slower. The Milky Way is also headed there, and that speed might be our fastest and primary direction.

Continuing the experiment, one would program the robotic positioning to move position every two minutes, or some such small time, and let the thing run itself for several months, return, analyze the data, find there were no anomalies, run it another six months, and maybe find something odd occurred during one two minute stop, bring up all the sensor data recordings from the event, calculate the exact position, the time it occurred, the day of the year, etc. Realistically one could try the same experiment on a miniaturized scale, with a three foot long bar of super conducting material, on a work bench. Three feet of travel is all that is involved, so a straight line for so short a distance.

I still get the distinct impression that the experiment might actually work. Acute sensors would pick up more static electricity when in alignment with the path we are traveling upon, since static electricity is not bound by gravity; the main problem is getting the two in alignment. Chances are the quantity of static electricity that could be captured wouldn't be enough to make it economically feasible to produce electricity on a large scale. But, if there is a small quantity there, and the true direction is found one time, it could be tracked, giving us every curve we follow.

The first positive reading gives experimenters a starting point, and losing track of the direction would thereafter be temporary, and eventually worked out over an extended period of time. Then, using the direction of things, which is then known, and numerous astronomical readings, a computer could triangulate the exact velocity of things in the Solar System, and stars in the galaxy. All one needs is time lapse to triangulate velocities. The question of the absolute frame of reference gets solved, except that the finding of the direction, a point from which velocity could be eventually calculated, is only by a stretch possible and in that manner technically difficult.

Static electricity may not be bound by gravity though that is debatable, but there is every reason to think that it would, upon its creation through friction, retain what inertia the things that created the static electricity possessed. In other words, static electricity, upon creation, isn't going to stop on a dime at that precise moment, it will continue along with all else. There might not be a small spike of electrical current along a length of super conducting material if it is lined up with the true direction of all things traveling in the vicinity.

One could argue that as time goes on, some static electricity could still accumulate in our wake. Those bits of static electricity already in existence, cast adrift with some inertia, eventually could fall behind the rapid progression of the Earth and Solar System. Supposing the Solar System and all in it are being pulled toward the "Deep Drift" object at an increasing speed, the static electricity, once it is on its own, won't be getting pulled there, and will slow down. Whether a larger amount of static electricity would be detectable along a straight length of super conducting material at only one particular direction of alignment isn't easy to tell. The scientists still being a little confused about gravity, it could turn out there isn't anything that is matter or energy that doesn't respond to gravitational forces. To the scientific community there doesn't appear to be a response to gravity in the case of lighter things, like light and static electricity, except near a black hole.

The "Deep Drift" object was in Centaurus, in the southern hemisphere of the sky. Where that is in relation to where an experiment is conducted might narrow the range a bit. Calculate what direction the Milky Way orbits the local cluster of galaxies, add where the Solar System is going as it orbits the Milky Way, and add that angle to the drift toward Centaurus, while factoring in Earth's spin on its axis, and yearly trip around the Sun.

The only other factor not taken into account would involve the motion of the largest entity of which we are a part, the known universe. Since the entire universe will doubtless be found to be in orbit in a universal plane, the entire known universe as a specific group of things traveling together in a loose sense will be in orbit in some specific direction quite unrelated to any other movements and also possibly faster than any of the other movements. The larger the object, or group of objects, the faster the orbit. To suppose the known universe is one super structure among an unknown number of other super structures with large black holes included in the vastness of space, seems to be a reasonable conclusion.

We could be orbiting the Milky Way somewhere around a half million miles an hour, but we could also be moving faster toward Deep Drift, 1,339,000 miles an hour or so, that being the speed of the Milky Way, and its likely destination. The known universe as a whole could have another destination. Without the least clue where we are in orbit around the entire universe, the fastest and most primary motion could be a complete mystery, and might counter to some extent other movements that are currently known. For example, the 500,000 mph that the Solar System travels around the Milky Way could be, sometimes, the exact opposite direction to the 1,399,000 mph of the Milky Way toward Deep Drift, and the motion of the known universe could be at right angles to those other two at that time.

All these motions would slowly change and thousands of years later those three motions would all stack up differently.

It could be that the accelerated expansion of the known universe has advanced to the point where it is no longer an isolated super structure with an orbit that all included within it follow, but is now several large super clusters of galaxies, with differing inertia, very far apart from other large super clusters.

It would be quite an accomplishment if the scientific community could solve the problem of the absolute frame of reference. Much more would be in our grasp were all sciences attuned to which way and how fast we are traveling through the universe. It could have implications in chemistry, new methods that would make it possible to make certain compounds more easily. Medical compounds once difficult to make become affordable to all. Micro-processor makers could make use of the absolute frame of reference to finely hone the internal components of computers. Any kind of nano type material or process involves very tiny things and events, and the absolute frame of reference could help in seeing how things could be more easily assembled on a small scale. The medical field may use the new information in making more specialized replacement organs.

Eventually, cell phones would have programs where the Absolute Frame of Reference could be accessed. Satellite and cell phone reception might require the cell phone user to be stationary on the planet. It would be quite difficult to triangulate absolute directions in space when cell phone user is traveling the Autobahn at speeds exceeding

100 mph. Friends throwing a Frisbee could pause, find the absolute frame of reference on a cell phone, and position themselves advantageously from the standpoint of the prevailing winds and direction through the void.

Soon after the blast of thunder in June, 1980 when I first realized these new possibilities I soon brought those copper coils outside to try to see what, if any, effect they might have, and these were dumb experiments too, because I had only 40 pounds of copper, and no real high place to put them. Even so, I think they contributed somewhat to the cloud development, and when I did place them outside some cloud development would occur, and seem to peak in intensity right around 72 hours after putting them out somewhere, and often look as though rain could come, but always little or none. I did add to it, over the early 80's, to where I was carrying around about 75 pounds of copper. I usually only ventured out when the forecasts called for cloudless skies.

All I can conclude now is that nothing I did at that time actually proved anything definitively, but I came to realize a path of least resistance does seem to be at the heart of the matter, involving water molecules and the primordial specks, and not N_2 and O_2, although the nitrogen and oxygen appear to become involved by way of gravity. I realized it would need a lot more copper by weight than what I was experimenting with back in the early 80's to produce a decent storm, and a higher location from whence they might broadcast waves a longer distance electromagnetically without obstruction.

I had seen what had happened in Texas, Australia, and Iowa where drought had ended suddenly shortly after my letters were sent there. I concluded those people must have tried a ton of copper on some hillside, maybe even two, doubting my assessment of the requirements. Copper was $1.50 a pound back then. Two tons of copper would have cost $6000, petty cash for a lot of wealthy corporations and people. I never advised anyone to try any more than 500 pounds, at least on the first try.

Perhaps this isn't the best time, dear.

It is also worth noting that when an experiment with copper on a hillside begins to bring about more and more quantities of water molecules and primordial specks, the H_2 in the water molecule is probably still capable of spawning further H even if connected to an oxygen atom. Such experiments would have brought together all the necessary ingredients for increased hydrogen production. Increased hydrogen production occurring in the atmosphere of the Earth would lead to more water molecules, as was observed previously, the rate dependent on how many hydrogen escape into outer space without meeting up with an oxygen atom.

Earlier, it was pointed out that should neutrons

result from the paired hydrogen atoms reproducing, about a fifteen minute delay would be involved in seeing the same effects as would occur if a fully fledged hydrogen atom, with an electron on the wing, were the product of the reproduction. Admittedly, I am not enough of a scientist to know for sure if neutrons created on Earth could join the nucleus of other atoms present. In an environment with less heat and pressure than found within a star, perhaps the electron shield of existing atoms in that environment preclude any neutrons from gaining entry. If neutrons could join existing atoms when newly created on Earth, if that transpires then less water molecules would emerge from hydrogen's reproductions, and more would have to be coming from evaporation in the oceans.

One could be sure not every neutron would find a home within an existing atom, and the majority would undergo beta decay where the electron and proton come apart. Then, the loose protons would still capture loose electrons and become single hydrogen atoms briefly before pairing up. A large percent of the newly nucleosynthesized entities could still wind up as part of a water molecule. An ozone layer trip being a half hour or more for newly created neutrons, most would rise and separate, combine anew into one hydrogen atom, find a mate, and from there become water, dependent upon how many new paired isotopes of hydrogen encounter free oxygen atoms in the ozone layer as they fly off the Earth and its atmosphere.

Maybe there aren't any accurate predictions to be made with quantities of copper beyond the 350 pounds at most that was used in my experiment. I haven't experimented in enough places or with enough copper to be making definitive statements, so the argument goes. Perhaps there are untold complications in some of the locations on Earth. Something is definitely happening when copper in the hundreds of pounds is placed on high. The only way to find out, for example, if the tornadoes in the middle of the country could be reduced or eliminated would be to conduct a few different experiments. Denying that copper so placed does anything delays the inevitable, the truth coming out, and getting put to appropriate use.

Chances are a location where 650 pounds of copper strategically located caused just the right sized storm to pass through, in a later trial with the same amounts of copper, different results were obtained. The first try was during a weather system quite different from the second one. A few hundred miles to the west, a large low pressure system was already in place on the second try, and with the added drop in barometric pressure from the copper of the second experiment, the storm system grew out of control. That type of thing can occur. Experimenters need to be aware of daily weather systems and factor in low pressure systems inbound. In this instance, the experimenters should have reduced the amount of copper by as much as a half to reduce the likelihood of disaster. Just how predictable these types of experiments can be will be found out as more experiments are tried.

Moving forward with something that offers new solutions to a plethora of problems with the Earth seems the best choice for humanity. Just because these atmospheric experiments involving copper have a point beyond which dangerous weather could occur and it is pretty easily reached, doesn't mean mankind couldn't live with it. We are already living with it; to continue to deny that dangerous weather could be man made, or might be avoided, is fatalistic. The idea is to promote the advantages of peaceful weather with abundant precipitation worldwide. Going with the idea puts one in the position of being able to do something about weather that is undesirable.

Needless to say, anecdotal evidence does not constitute proof. However, when there is a preponderance of events where an experiment appeared to have been attempted, and each of those events saw a change from a drought situation to a condition where water became abundant quickly, one should, at least, begin to wonder. The properties of the water molecule being such as has been shown more likely at the bottom of it all, or at least the most significant factor, it makes me wonder how someone who has read all that has been presented here could conclude otherwise than the author.

For 30 years and more I have been curious about what interested me in the summer of 1980, a path of least resistance being created by a quantity of copper in a high location. The conclusion reached is precipitation is easily obtained virtually anywhere on Earth, in any season. The process is as tested, tried, and true as any cautious investigator with limited resources could determine. Extrapolating that lead would have the opposite effect is not unreasonable. What happens from this point on in the world should be an improvement. Steering clear of weather disasters will one day be the norm.

Chapter 10: Suppositions and Predictions

Garden of Eden Hasn't Happened Yet

JB

Last but not least, a full record of the entire Primordial Speck Theory needs to be written up, with its suppositions and predictions. That way, we can all see in the fullness of time whether the predictions are fulfilled, and if the suppositions it makes hold true. One day maybe more sensitive equipment will be designed that will distinguish three or four different particles in random space that prior to that time were below the threshold of detection.

If that happens, then a one particle hydrogen precursor theory would obviously be wrong, and not stand the test of time. Most suppositions made by the theory would all probably still hold even if the number of very small things was more than one type. The varying types would combine in whatever way to become hydrogen whatever the dark matter and dark energy are, and we are currently in a position where only theory will shed any light. For the sake of simplicity the theory goes with one fundamental particle, since the most pulverized thing possible doesn't seem likely to have choices.

Supposition 1: That undetected dark matter and dark energy in the known universe are primordial specks, precursors to hydrogen made of matter and energy too small to detect, probably one fundamental particle in astounding abundance.

Supposition 2: That these primordial specks are most likely magnetic monopoles. When primordial specks are in sufficient concentrations they change into hydrogen through the stable hydrogen isotope, H_2, serving as a template. Two H atoms together produce another proton and electron from smaller particles. Chances are we will never know what size each individual primordial speck is, nor the steps it takes to unite with others and become a hydrogen atom, comprised of a proton with three quarks within, and an electron in orbit about it. Changes are somehow incorporated into very, very small things in the space between two identical hydrogen atoms that assume the shape of a larger thing, becoming a unity. That unity is a neutron, or a hydrogen atom. In either case, an increase in hydrogen in the early universe would have resulted; once stars begin to unite in nuclear fusion, and heavier elements get created, neutrons could do other things than decay into a proton and electron. Nevertheless, each additional neutron created adds to the percentage of matter and energy that is known, and takes away from that which is dark.

Supposition 3: Being magnetic monopoles, primordial specks are unstable and energetic. They will accumulate along a path of least resistance such as can be created by placing a quarter ton of copper as earlier specified near a mountain top facing the prevailing westerlies.

Supposition 4: The accumulation of primordial specks in increased concentrations along a path of least resistance and the nucleosynthesis of hydrogen in the atmosphere will result in newly formed hydrogen atoms pairing up as stable H2 isotopes, rising to the ozone layer, joining with a free oxygen atom there, and in great quantities becoming water molecules that join developing clouds. If neutrons are the created product, a quarter hour delay results in the same events, hydrogen atoms joining with an oxygen atom, in the ozone layer.

Supposition 5: The primordial specks gathering in increasing numbers along a path of least resistance, traveling in the same direction, along with water molecules, will pull the electrically inert N_2 and O_2 that accounts for 99% of the air along with them gravitationally along the path of least resistance. The other 1% of the known air, argon, methane, neon, carbon dioxide, etc., will follow the pull of the mass of the water molecules and primordial specks, and join the schooling cascade. All this results in falling barometric pressure, cloud accumulation and precipitation, usually around 72 hours into the experiment. Supposition 4 also figures into the clouds and precipitation.

Supposition 6: The combination of suppositions 4 and 5 along with some other additional factors helping such as the jet stream, static electricity, magnetic field changes, etc., proves that a path of least resistance can be created with a row of copper tubing in a high location, resulting, if the experiment is properly conducted and not ruined by other nearby experiments, in precipitation occurring 72 hours, give or take 8 hours, into the experiment. Also that cloud development will start promptly within an hour or two of insertion of copper of sufficient size near a mountain top, and build in intensity until the release occurs in the form of rainfall. The polar nature of the water molecule may prove to be the most decisive factor in producing the effects described, but probably isn't enough by itself.

Supposition 7: That since we have established that dark energy and dark matter is in the form of particulates that are a combination of both matter and energy, the excess of the dark energy over dark matter can be explained by the 52% excess dark energy consisting of the gravitational pull of massive objects further from us than the known universe. This gives us 90 to 92 percent of all in the known universe being primordial specks and 8 to 10 percent being known matter, hydrogen on up the elements, some neutrinos, and released energy from matter in various forms.

The increased acceleration of the known universe is explained by this and it is predicted that other objects of mass will be found outside the known universe. This may have already happened over the last few years with recent astronomical discoveries that now are still being investigated, so my thinking is that the two recent science articles about things possibly outside the known universe will eventually be confirmed. Right now the idea that 52% of the dark energy is in the form of distant objects converts the dark energy into things, then, that are a combination of matter and energy, just like here, it is simply that we are getting no information from them other than gravitational pull. The mass of the hypothesized more distant objects have never gone in to calculations because we have no way currently of finding it out. We only have the strength of a force trying to pull the known universe apart.

Supposition 8: That space has not, as is thought by many, been shown to admit of alteration. That photons, a form of energy with no mass, should be bent by massive objects in their vicinity, proves nothing other than that the photons changed course, not that the space changed. It would be ludicrous to suppose that light waves fail to escape a black hole due to a change in space, when it is clearly intense gravitational collapse of a massive thing responsible. A more thorough theory of gravity with space as a fabric thrown out will emerge from this within 20 years. Space will be concluded to be an increate void, and it would be impossible to remove nothingness from somewhere.

Supposition 9: Particles do not pop out of zero point energy or some such things, they coalesce into hydrogen from smaller particles probably within a stable hydrogen isotope. Primordial specks will in time be concluded to exist, and be regarded as the most abundant thing in the universe by almost all literate people in 40 years.

Supposition 10: Given the truth of Supposition 7, the known universe is not the entire universe. Given that, our known universe need not collapse back in on itself, and the accelerated expansion of the universe will continue, and eventually the cold, lifeless things that were once our solar system will be absorbed by a black hole, which will eventually collide with another, creating more billions of galaxies, so the universe will always exist, and we will never know its full size.

Supposition 11: That an experiment with copper in a high location, yielding greater concentrations of primordial specks would show more hydrogen atoms in random air samples taken 72 into the experiment than an experiment of the same type that instead used a row of lead sheets positioned from north to south facing the prevailing westerlies, with air samples taken 72 hours into the lead experiment of identical size as the other.

For successful tests of that prediction, however, one must know that in the copper part of the experiment, the barometric pressure will in all likelihood be much lower, the relative humidity much higher, and it will probably be raining. Thus, some of the hydrogen found at that moment might have come from a water molecule falling apart, so one would have to factor in an estimated amount of those. I really don't know if water molecules break apart easily or not. One might wonder how many water molecules have brand new H_2 isotopes, but finding that out is not possible.

It is predicted that numerous experiments of the type mentioned will be carried out, and evidence that additional hydrogen is present in greater parts per billion in the copper part of the experiment beyond an amount correctly calculated for water molecules coming apart will happen within 30 years.

Suppositions 12: Within 30 years, an experiment with copper in a high location with a vacuum chamber nearby will discover additional hydrogen in the vacuum chamber after it had been placed, with some hydrogen atoms within to serve as templates, at the site of the experiment with copper. A similar experiment with a vacuum chamber that had been emptied as much as possible of the same size will not be found to contain any additional hydrogen. This will prove without a doubt that new hydrogen requires already existing hydrogen pairs to serve as a template, and also proves hydrogen production in the early universe began slowly, and is now still ongoing, mostly within stars.

Supposition 13: During the last three decades of the 21st century, a mathematician will calculate exactly the smallest magnetic monopole that can possibly be made, and computer simulations with new data inputted for the mass of the primordial specks will show accuracy predicting actual conditions. With the new information as to the size of each magnetic monopole and the need of H_2 templates for hydrogen nucleosynthesis to occur, the rate of hydrogen production will be calculated and found to be still taking place.

Supposition14: The storms that brew over the oceans and are known by the names typhoon, hurricane, and cyclone could be wholly erased if mankind worked with each other and diverted a substantial portion of the water vapor and static electricity out over the oceans towards land. Additional drainage of the oceans could be accomplished by positioning more than the usual amount of copper near the north and south poles. This last mentioned activity would also rebuild the polar ice caps. The prediction is a sharp falling off of such storms in the next two decades.

Supposition 15: Tornadoes could be reduced to somewhere around a 98% year to year decrease, with a little experimentation with various ways of creating a path of least resistance. It is predicted that the prevalence of tornadoes will fall off sharply within two decades. Flooding and drought also become much less trouble in the next two decades. It is predicted that a barometric pressure hot line will come into being sometime in the next 20 years. It is also predicted that this hot line will no longer exist in 50 years, along with the weather channel.

Supposition 16: The insurance industry and branches of government in the United States will revise the term “Acts of God” to “Acts of Nature With Possible Human Involvement“, or some other more accurate term when referring to weather events by the end of the 21st century.

Supposition 17: Since we have restored space to her former glory, and space/time being a mistaken idea, or something applicable to equations but not reality, then the Big Bang didn't occur as theorists now maintain it did with space/time collapsing into a point together with all the mass of the entire universe contained within, but was more likely the collision of two super massive black holes, in an empty quadrant of the much larger universe, since these two black holes that collided soaked up the matter in the area to a distance of 10 billion light years in every direction before colliding, but a trail of particles likely followed both black holes as each accelerated for each other, including hydrogen pairs. It is predicted that Einstein's theories will still hold, with the condition that time may be variable, but space is not.

Supposition 18: Computer simulations with the suppositions listed above will yield an accurate picture of reality, and be able to predict weather conditions 72 hours into the future within a small variable, since no two storms are exactly alike, and the complex system of the atmosphere on Earth can have accurate predictions made about it, despite whatever chaos theory may say to the contrary.

Supposition19: Global warming within 30 years is no longer viewed as an imminent threat. Global temperatures stabilize within that time and begin to show little variation from year to year, with ocean levels below the highs of thirty years before.

Supposition20: The increased availability of water on land, and improved runoff from rivers to oceans begins to slow the extinction of species considerably in 20 years. The plant and animal life in the wild on land and in oceans and fresh water habitats begins to show marked increases in populations in 30 years.

Supposition21: Desalinization plants will no longer be planned in twenty years, and in the case of those already existing, some are decommissioned and converted to sports stadiums within twenty years.

Supposition22: Within fifty years, an attempt to harvest electricity from lightning will have been made, and based upon actual data from the ongoing project, many small weather making stations built to capture electricity will spring up around the world. By the end of the 21st century the number of such weather modification stations equipped to capture lightning and convert it into electrical current while producing adequate precipitation for the local area it occupies exceeds 100.

Supposition23: The encyclopedia of the world will begin to have information about the type of weather modification discussed in this book within 20 years.

Supposition 24: The Absolute Frame Of Reference will be worked out by astronomers within the next 50 years. Set to the task of finding our direction through empty space by sheer accident, a computer program is developed that has 10 second time lapse astronomical movies stored. Then the computer is set to the task of finding the straight line that the Earth moved along during that 10 second event. The program compares billions of possible directions through space per second and eventually finds which direction matched astronomical readings. Having comparisons with which to reduce error, and after having worked out the direction of the Earth through space, the computer then works out where that direction is, and how it changes.

CONCLUSION

Difference Between Success And Failure.
But The Wand Is Too Big.
JB

This process in nature that I've tried to show and talk up needs a full investigation by the scientific community. I watched the presentation about Ardi, the 4.4 million year old hominid fossil found in the highlands of Ethiopia, and all the nations and scientists who collaborated in the find, and excavation and examination of the fossil, and it seems a good deal of time and trouble was spent on it. Some time and trouble could easily be spent in investigating the processes described in this book.

I referred to that archeological find in the introduction of this book. That television show I watched broke a long standing paradigm. The mainstream archeological community had long discounted hominid finds made that appeared to be from a time longer ago than 100,000 years, and the predisposition of most archeologists to ignore older finds became the subject of a book. Forbidden Archeology[11] by Michael A. Cremo and Richard L. Thompson explores a number of archeological discoveries swept under the rug.

That book was a more challenging bit of work, and the authors did a great job. Archeology and meteorology have both developed problems with discerning the truth as it applies to its particular discipline. It seems to have paid off if popular television carries an archeology program about a much older hominid fossil than previously. The paradigm shifted, in less than 15 years from the publication of Forbidden Archeology. This book doesn't have the wealth of research Forbidden Archeology has, but cosmology and astrophysics differ from archeology. There are no specimens in sciences that deal with hypothetical questions.

Meteorology differs quite a bit from archeology as well. There are things to study in meteorology, one real possibility uncatalogued that needs more light shed on it. My hope is this book will help to serve as an impetus to move this idea further along, similarly to what happened in archeology. One would think that meteorology would get a more careful review, and more details about what has been discussed about weather modification should see a presentation on public television.

The scientific community could expand on this issue to the point where my book here would look like an introduction. The resources and technicians the scientific community has could answer all the questions raised herein and give much more detail about these issues. Readers can help the author to see more development in this area just by being of that opinion. If enough people insist on wanting to see further investigation into something, it one day happens. An episode of "Mythbusters" some day might investigate the possibility that passive placement of pure metals in large quantities in a high location could do things to the weather.

People like to know things. I believe that there is something to what I have tried to present. The invisible forces of electromagnetism and gravity are all around us continually; that the two combine to produce effects involving the water molecule, along with the hypothesized primordial specks such as described makes sense. It fits all the data. The seeing is conceptual with the primordial specks, and the forces of nature.

No other explanation or theory fits all the facts as well. Contemplating how dangerous activity like this could be, it doesn't get any more or any less dangerous based on how many people on Earth know of it, it is an inescapable feature of having a tool capable of doing as described. Knowing always involves a kind of empowerment, and, surely, once enough people become aware of this and begin to discuss it, our birth as weather modifiers will begin, and before long, management of fresh water on a worldwide basis will come easily and safely.

All humanity needs to do is get this confirmed by reputable scientists and placed in encyclopedia. Self-preservation will take it from there. We have a low-tech tool with a wide range of uses, some of which were mentioned earlier. There is some work involved with using the tool, some equipment, some high places required to place things, but surely possible almost anywhere on the globe.

If weather events in the future will be done by nature alone, or with some assistance, won't be easy to ascertain in a world where humans don't learn this. That world will be a world where this feature, this process in nature, will still exist, acknowledged or not. The beauty of nature stands a chance only if weather is optimized for the wild inhabitants. Traveling through Yellowstone National Park about a decade ago we saw a Yellowstone with huge tracts of scorched trees, from forest fires not long before. My appreciation of nature was not helped by the destruction caused by unrestrained mother nature. Firefighters and equipment, planes and helicopters dumping chemicals and water were used to fight the fires, surely, but that is hardly the most effective way to combat a forest fire.

Weather disasters need to be reclassified. The possibility that these types of misfortune could be minimized, even eliminated completely, exists. No one is going to try to minimize a possible weather disaster if one appears likely without knowledge of how to do so. Proof would be needed. One wouldn't base actions on unproven information, which is what this is without science confirming.

Science and applied science are two different things. One would have to group the process of placing metals on hills into the applied science category. That doesn't change things much, since encyclopedia already have the term "weather modification" among subjects in encyclopedia. There is a place for a summary of the processes presented in this book.

Supposing weather problems with flooding got out of control by 1930, it is possible that whoever was experimenting at the time decided that the whole process was too dangerous, and kept the matter to themselves. I think it likely something of the sort took place. A group of meteorologists, the Army Corps of Engineers, even some group like the Freemasons might have been doing the experimenting. Were it these last, secrecy is part of the agenda of that group. In that day and age it may have been possible to keep one of the more significant discoveries of modern times from public knowledge. Indeed, it happened, for the process has not yet found the encyclopedia.

Today, numerous satellites constantly view every inch of Earth from space. The internet connects every corner of the world to every other corner.

The exact wrong thing to do in this day and age would be to try to continue to keep this a secret. Empowering everyone will eventually take away any plausible deniability when it comes to playing with the weather. Weather modification attempts would be strictly controlled and monitored before long, once the initial idea gains acceptance.

Currently the weather is viewed as occurring naturally; I can't prove that some of the odd weather that has occurred recently has been anything but that. Continuing to view the weather as occurring naturally in the future, in light of all that has been presented, would be foolish in the extreme. It would be extremely helpful if one day some weather modification activity that got out of hand involving a man made metal deposit actually got found and removed by the authorities, preventing a weather disaster. If some event like that were to occur, and then be discussed, it might start a change of attitude, a bit more optimism about the whole idea.

The number of meteorologists, hydrologists, electrical engineers, horticulturists and other professional people who could have this knowledge available to them is staggering. Bringing flooding under control in this day and age should be considerably easier than it was in 1930. Since that is the only impediment to learning of this process, experiments with lead to raise air pressure should be explored as soon as possible. Negatively charged electromagnets could prove effective in repelling water molecules, as well. Finding copper or lead or an electromagnet that is causing trouble, in this day, is going to be a lot easier than it was years ago. If the governing body got serious about a zero tolerance policy toward weather tampering, SWAT teams could be descending from helicopters upon a location with falling pressure in a few hours. It would help if laws were passed before drastic measures are taken. Debate, and trial and error experiments should get us closer to the truth in this matter.

The general public should be the agency that makes the decision in a free society about the comparative safety of learning a process and remaining ignorant. My contention is that the public is the supreme ruler of the marketplace. The minority that may do mischief are overrun by all the professional people able to put these processes to productive and safe use. No group will keep mankind in the dark like the last century.

Dangers being possible with the kind of activity discussed here, and the difficulties involved in getting a scientific discipline to change its stance regarding new discoveries, the paradigm may not shift for a long time. Who knows when these new ideas reach an encyclopedia. That is up to the youth of the world, and upcoming generations. They will not be starting with as little as I did. One book points the way. No human wants to live like a horse, with blinders preventing them from seeing the big picture. Seeing the big picture is going to be hard without reputable scientific help.

To recount, 1910 or thereabouts a precedent was set whereby this discovery is discounted in scientific journals. That has continued to this day, and present day scientists are not to blame either, since the paradigm is so ingrained in just about everyone after all this time that no one felt it necessary to look any closer. The author has followed a well worn path, though, and anyone could have done so decades before me.

I'd like to include a conceivable excerpt from a future hypothetical encyclopedia.... Weather Modification; Any act or process created by human activity that has as its end result the changing of the weather. Recent discoveries show weather systems can be created and destroyed by placing purified copper or lead in quantity in a high location. Copper tends to lower barometric pressure and produce storms, and lead seems to have the opposite effect. The storms brought on by copper in a high location usually take 72 hours to develop give or take 8 hours. Places near an ocean to the west could see precipitation 12 hours sooner than places further inland. Why these effects should happen isn't precisely certain, but much of the effects are probably due to the polar nature of the water molecule, and maybe some primordial specks from the Big Bang cruising the path of least resistance provided by the copper along with the water molecules. Lead seems to provide no particle with charge any clear path to follow, and scattering of particles in the vicinity of lead in a high location raises air pressure, dispersing clouds.

Electromagnets proved too unpredictable, but can also attract or repel water molecules, depending on the polarity. The authorities of most countries are these days quite adamant that no experiments of these types be conducted by anyone simply curious about the process. Meteorological communities worldwide have all banded together to try to see that as few weather disasters as possible is the norm, so don't try this for yourself! If you feel your area is not receiving sufficient precipitation, or too much precipitation, consult the nearest Chamber of Commerce. For further reading see; Water Experiments, Weather Knowledge, Weather Laws, Water Engineering, WAFT.

Any rational being, having read the arguments put forth here, would see that it is our duty in the natural scheme of things to perform custodial work on the planet that we live on. Had humans not arisen as the creature at the apex of life on this planet, some other animal would have after a while, and so, in the cosmic scheme of things, a creature at the top of the food chain will evolve, and fill the position of the only creature on the planet capable of modifying the weather. The universe doesn't expect that creature to carry out this duty. The universe just makes it possible.

* References

1. Tesla: Man Out Of Time
   By Margaret Cheney C.1981
2. Tesla: Man Out Of Time
   By Margaret Cheney C.1981
3. Giant Molecules, Here, There, and Evrywhere
   By Alexander Yu. Grosberg and
   Alexei R. Khokhlov C.1997
4. Dark Cosmos; In Search Of Our Universe's
   Missing Mass and Energy
   By Dan Hooper C.2006
5. Dark Cosmos; In Search Of Our Universe's
   Missing Mass and Energy
   By Dan Hooper C.2006
6. Dark Cosmos; In Search Of Our Universe's
   Missing Mass and Energy
   By Dan Hooper C.2006
7. Weather Modification by Cloud Seeding
   By Arnett S. Dennis C.1980
   Weather and Climate Modification:
   Problems and Progress
   By Thomas F. Malone C.1980
   Weather Modification: Prospects and Problems
   By Georg Breuer C.1980
8. Human Action C. 1949
   By Ludwig Von Mises
9. Atlas Shrugged
   By Ayn Rand C.1957
10. Modern Physics and Antiphysics
    By Adolph Baker C.1970
11. Forbidden Archeology
    By Michael A. Cremo and
    Richard L. Thompson C.1993

INDEX

A

B

INDEX

INDEX

INDEX

S

T

INDEX

U

V

W

X

Y